Ollie Tibbles

Ollie Tibbles

The Boy Who Became a Train

Debi Tibbles

MEDALLION
P R E S S
Medallion Press, Inc.

Printed in USA

For Ollie.

Love you always and forever.

Mummy

Special thanks to Metra

and the Make-A-Wish Foundation.

Published 2012 by Medallion Press, Inc.

The MEDALLION PRESS LOGO
is a registered trademark of Medallion Press, Inc.

Typeset in Adobe Garamond Pro
Printed in the United States of America

ISBN# 978160542491

10 9 8 7 6 5 4 3 2 1
First Edition

CONTENTS

Foreword

We are sitting on the deck attached to the small home in Michigan's Upper Peninsula as the late summer evening begins to descend on our conversation. It has been all about life lessons, how they show up and perhaps why, and other events in our lives that leave no explanation and even fewer clues. I study the impending sunset that is painting the last clouds of the day in a hue from the palette that only the architect of the universe can claim as Debi sits back and says, "Even with all the bloody pain in the world, life is still worth it."

She would know.

My mind races back three years to the first time my path crossed with Debi's. I was attending a fund-raiser at the Lincoln Park Zoo in Chicago, and after a full day of rain the evening promised to be glorious. As I made my way past the silent auction tables and toward the main dining room, I noticed a woman standing near the bar area. She appeared to be a female version of rocker Billy Idol—her hair was spiked up and snow-white, various tattoos adorned her formidable arms, and she was in all black.

Two weeks later I came into my office in Chicago, and sitting in the foyer was "Billy Idol" from the event!

I said, "I know you!"

She countered, "The bloody hell you do?"

Debi and I have been friends ever since.

Ollie Tibbles: The Boy Who Became a Train is not just a book . . . it's a miracle in the making. It's a story that will test every belief you have about what is possible, how unbearable pain can be transformed into incredible possibility, and what it takes to live your truth. Through the loss of her son, Debi found her voice by taking a journey that no parent wants to embark on—ever.

Having a front row seat to the Debi Tibbles Experience, I have watched her move in directions no one could have predicted, standing up when so many sit down, and moving ahead when it would be so easy to sit back. Courage can be defined in many ways, but for me it means listening within when all around you seem to hold you back and breaking through the walls you've built so one day you have the satisfaction of finding your true self.

When my day gets heavy or my thoughts of my own losses are too much to bear, I think of Debi plowing through the darkest days imaginable and my load seems much lighter. If I need more of a kick I will ring her up, and all it takes is that "Hello, Big Man, how are you?" and I am back . . . on track.

I pray that someday after reading this book you, too, have a chance to meet this very special person who carries on a promise she made to her young son Ollie, whom she misses more than life itself—a promise Debi shares with you as you embark on this journey. It's a ride you will never forget.

John St. Augustine
Rapid River, Michigan
August 2010

John St. Augustine has been called "the voice of America" by veteran broadcaster Charles Osgood and "the most influential voice on radio" by best-selling author Cheryl Richardson. He was the creator and host of Power!Talk Radio, a nationally syndicated radio show, and executive producer of

The Dr. Oz Show on Oprah & Friends on XM Satellite Radio. He is the best-selling author of *Living an Uncommon Life* (2006) and *Every Moment Matters* (2009).

Introduction

My name is Debi Tibbles, and I am English. I love Marmite and fish-and-chips—old style, newspapers and all with malt vinegar and a big, fat Wally, please! I say, "Bloody hell," a lot and possess a saucy sense of humor. I share this with you now, especially if you are American, so that you are prepared for the onslaught of all things British in me as you turn these pages.

I am also the proud mother of Jessica, George, and Ollie, my greatest achievements.

Despite generous words to the contrary from those who have already read my story, I never considered myself a writer, never imagined I'd actually write a book, yet I believe there's a story in all of us. Some of us get to see it come alive within pages, while others of us see it only in our dreams. This story is not a work of fiction; it really happened. And while I know I won't receive any literary prizes, I stand firm in the belief that what you are about to read is the greatest prize I could ever receive and share with you. Through the eyes of a child, my child, you will be afforded heartache, joy, and inspiration—and an opportunity to meet a clown in a white coat.

I could say to you that this is a mother's story, my own story, and it is. Yet it is more than that. It is everyone's story. It's the unwritten story we all have embedded within but have forgotten about or perhaps ignored. For me, it's a story that was all of these things and more, and it was certainly not my idea to share it. Credit for that goes to my son Ollie, who strongly felt it should be shared—and he always was a persistent little bugger. With that cute, cheeky monkey grin of his, how could I refuse?

Welcome, My Son

The mellow tones of The Eagles' "Tequila Sunrise" drifted through my headset as I climbed another torturous mountain of pain, my labor reaching its peak.

I was amazingly calm as I wondered for the umpteenth time about the child within me: a boy or a girl? I had no clue and was not one of those mothers who liked to know during pregnancy. I had relished the not knowing, the guessing, the talks in the bathtub with my yet unborn child. "Well, hello, little man—or are you a little girl?" I'd say, mesmerized by the faint outline of a little fist pushing toward my voice.

I'd been spot-on with Jess, our first, and with George, our second. Jess had been almost ladylike as she'd squirmed and wriggled, stretching like an elegant ballerina. She had entered the world crying pitifully. George had enjoyed the occasional game of soccer in my womb, throwing in a bit of boxing just for the hell of it. He had entered the world yelling his head off. Who knew a pair of lungs just a few seconds old could project so?

Teetering on the edge, I knew my climb was over. I could feel the urgency and desperate need to push as my body succumbed to its natural state. It was time. I could hardly believe I was there already. It had only taken me two hours to climb that mountain. With a gut-wrenching scream, I pushed and my newborn child silently and calmly entered the light and the waiting arms of the midwife.

I eagerly reached for my child and held him close, savoring each minute, adoring the tiny being with a mass of dark hair. As my warm, wet baby squirmed on my chest, I beheld his tiny perfect fingers and toes, his adorable little bottom, and his delightful pert nose. As he attempted to open his eyes, he did not yell or cry but merely whimpered, screwing up his beautiful, wrinkled face. He was offended, it seemed, to have been evicted from his lovely, warm place inside my belly.

Smiling, I felt a surge of overwhelming love, my soul speaking to his: *Oh, precious child, my beautiful son, so this is who you are. Oh, how I love you. Welcome to this wonderful world and all that awaits you.* Gazing at him, I knew him immediately. "Welcome, Oliver," I whispered. "Welcome, my Ollie. May all your dreams come true . . ."

CHAPTER 1
Listening to the Voice

I picked up the phone and recognized the voice of Missy, the school secretary at Willow Creek Elementary, where our children attended. Which one might need me: our ten-year-old Jess, seven-year-old George, or five-year-old Ollie? It was Ollie, who was complaining of a headache and wanted to come home.

I hung up, cursing under my breath that I'd have to cancel my hair appointment.

In the school's sick bay next to the office, however, my concern quickly shifted. Ollie lay on the bed, face crumpled with pain, hands cradling his head. Tears slowly rolled down his cheeks as he looked up. "Mummy, my head. My head, Mummy." His arms reached for me.

Seeing his pain, I scooped him up and whispered in his ear as I carried him out of the school building. "It's okay, baby. It's okay. Mummy's here. Shhh."

My words of comfort were in vain. In obvious agony, he started to wail.

This was not the first time Ollie had gotten a bad headache. In fact, he'd been having them on a fairly regular basis. I assumed he suffered from migraines, just as I had as a child.

He held me tightly, still clutching his head. "Mummy, my head *hurts*. Make it stop."

Though I was alarmed, I tried to reassure him as I put him in the car. Every time we drove over a bump, I winced, aware of his pain.

His wails continued during a short yet excruciatingly long drive home.

When we entered the garage, without warning Ollie started vomiting. I was taken aback by the sheer violence of it. He looked terrified, his eyes bulging. He was trying to speak but didn't have time. His little body was shaking uncontrollably, the vomit exploding relentlessly from his wide-open mouth.

The bathroom was just around the corner. Why hadn't he waited? Usually if the kids felt sick, they would first tell me, hold it, then run to the bathroom. As Ollie stood doubled over, one hand on the door, one hand clutching his stomach, I finally realized what he was trying to say: he was sorry for messing the kitchen floor.

I gulped, stopping myself from crying. "Baby, don't be silly. I don't care about the floor." Between eruptions, I wiped his nose and mouth clean.

After what seemed an age, the vomiting ceased. Glancing at the clock, I realized the whole episode had lasted almost fifteen minutes.

Immediately, however, the severe pain in his head returned. His outcries resumed.

I gave him Tylenol and sat with him until he finally fell into a deep sleep that lasted hours.

The fact that Ollie slept so long should have alarmed me. This was not what a normal, healthy, robust five-year-old would do. As soon as children are able to move, there's no stopping them—and Ollie was no exception. The youngest of our three children, he'd walked early and was soon skipping, running, and jumping his way into trouble in his adorable way.

I'll never forget the time I found him perched on an upside-down plastic toy container on the kitchen counter, a chair atop as his stairway to heaven: namely, the sweetie cupboard. His head was buried in a bag of Tootsie Rolls before he looked at me proudly with his *See what I can do?* grin.

"You cheeky monkey," I said, using our pet name for Ollie and picking him up for a huge cuddle.

We had terms of endearment reflecting each of our kids' unique personalities. Jess was the minx, George was the little monster, and Ollie, who'd mischievously been into everything since he could crawl, was our cheeky monkey.

Our cheeky monkey was not himself. Over the course of several weeks, Ollie had another episode and then another, and my fear set in. Something was seriously wrong. I sensed it. The natural instinct of a mother was warning me, and the feeling would not go away.

I called Peter, who was working on an assignment in London. I told him my concerns for our son, yet I was torn about truly sharing what I felt, not wanting to worry him.

Frightened of what it all meant, I pushed it to the back of my mind, turning instead to comforting thoughts: *He'll be fine. You'll see. It's just severe migraines. There has to be something else going on because, after all, nothing that bad could ever happen to us.*

Oh, the bliss of ignorance.

I could not have been more wrong. As the weeks passed with Ollie's episodes rendering him unable to go to school, I finally listened to the voice within and took him to our doctor.

Sitting in the doctor's waiting room, I watched Ollie play with his Thomas the Tank Engine trains, weaving in and out of the chairs.

Ollie's passion for trains had begun as soon as he'd been able to hold toys and books in his little hands.

When we lived in London, we used both the Underground (The Tube) and also Main Line trains to get around. He knew every kind of engine, what *switches* and *buffers* referred to, what a turntable was, the difference between certain train depots and how each one was used. Nothing brought this home to him more than the stories of Thomas & Friends, and he had them all, along with the videos, coloring books, bed linens, and clothing.

Ollie's interest continued to grow after we arrived in Chicago. When he was around the age of five, we took him to our local station in Downers Grove where he saw the Metra passenger train for the first time and was completely transfixed.

"It's a double-decker—like our red buses in England, Mummy!"

In a way, he was right. Little did I know just how significant this particular train would be to us.

"Toot, toot!" Ollie yelled joyfully in the doctor's waiting room. It had been just over a week since his last episode, and he was doing fine.

Everything was back to normal, so what was I doing here? This was just a waste of time, and I might as well leave. Yet in the pit of my stomach the constant nagging wouldn't go away.

Ollie, on the other hand, was blissfully unaware and continued to play happily, crawling along the floor, choo-chooing loudly, much to the annoyance of his fellow patients in the waiting room. A rather grim-faced lady politely asked me to keep my son quiet, and I apologized. It was the last time I would ever apologize for my son.

Our family doctor was a kind, pleasant man whom we all felt comfortable around. Ollie giggled as he prodded his belly during the examination.

He asked lots of questions. "How many headaches does he get a month?"

"Three to four."

"Does he always vomit when he gets a headache?"

"He didn't at first, but he does now."

"Is he having problems with his vision?"

"I never even thought about that, but actually yes." Sometimes Ollie would get double vision or, in his own words, "see two of everything." When he put his hand up to cover one eye, it helped him see properly.

"Does that happen a lot?"

"No, just now and again."

"Does he eat a lot of chocolate?"

"What? Of course! He's a kid."

"Do the headaches come after he eats chocolate?"

"Ummm, sometimes."

"And after he eats cheese?"

It just so happened that Ollie ate a lot of both.

"Do you think we should get an MRI done?" I said hesitantly. "You know, just in case?" I didn't even know why I asked. The question had seemed to just pop into my head.

He assured me that there was no reason for concern and that Ollie was probably experiencing these headaches due to food allergies. It was common, apparently. He suggested natural products for Ollie without additives, and I said we'd give them a try.

I felt relieved, comforted by all he said. Surely the doctor would know of any signs of something more serious, wouldn't he? Once more, I tried to put the fears away.

When I arrived home I got on the phone to Pete to relay what the doctor had said. He sounded miserable. He was lonely. Despite being employed here in Chicago, the company needed him at the London branch for a while, and even though he enjoyed working with old colleagues and seeing friends and family on a regular basis, he missed us all, especially the kids. He would make trips back home once a month. It was a challenging time for him, and he was doing his best to adjust.

It was sometimes hard for me as well. Life alone with the kids was often chaotic as I juggled school, homework, activities, and time with them, often without a break. I had a new-found admiration for single mothers. I was tired often, and I realized with a pang of guilt that I missed my freedom while Pete was away more than I missed him. I missed adult conversations, ones that did not revolve around SpongeBob's latest antics or what the Teletubbies were making for lunch.

Teaching group fitness became my salvation on the rare days I got out of the house. Freedom! That's how I perceived it at the time.

I didn't empathize with how Pete was feeling. He was lonely, yet selfishly I didn't see it that way. I could only think of how things were for me. During our conversations, without thinking, I would focus more on how I was coping, the old *pity me* syndrome. Only when he mentioned how much he missed the kids would I wake out of my selfish fog and truly listen to what he was saying.

He was just as worried as I was about Ollie, yet like me he felt comforted to hear what the doctor had said. After chatting about his health for a while, he agreed that we should see how things were once we changed his diet. After all, he was fine now and maybe it had been merely allergies all along. No worries.

I pushed all thoughts about Ollie's health to the back of my mind as the conversation shifted to the family vacation we were planning. We would stay in Pete's fancy apartment in the heart of London for three weeks in March.

The kids and I had been counting down the days. Seeing Pete again would be fun. He was my best friend, the guy I could say anything to, the one who understood me and could always make me laugh.

Also, I was hoping this trip would rekindle something in our marriage. I hoped that absence really would make the heart grow fonder and we could find ourselves again.

As I hung up, I was hopeful.

‿◦⊱❀⊰◦‿

I awoke to screaming and a strange gurgling sound.

A frightened George yelled at the top of his voice, "Mummy, come quick!" A pause, then, "Mum! *Mummy!*"

I leapt out of bed, my heart pounding, and sprinted to the boys' room directly across the hall. Jess came out, all bleary-eyed, then immediately awake as Ollie let out another terrifying scream.

George stood at the end of Ollie's bed, watching almost trancelike as Ollie's projectile vomit hit the floor and sprayed George's bed on the other side of the room. I'll never forget the look on his face: pure terror.

I tried to stay calm.

"It's okay, Georgie. Ollie's got an upset tummy. He'll be okay. Go get a bucket and a flannel for me, okay? And thank you, sweetie, for calling me."

I knelt by Ollie's bed as he lay half out of it.

Vomit covered his pillow, bed, and pajamas. He was sweating profusely and holding his head.

I tried to clean him up, whispering, "It's okay, baby. It's okay. Shhh, Mummy's here," as I picked up globs of puke and threw them in the bucket George handed to me.

There was a pause, and then Ollie cried out in a voice I had not heard before, a terrible, almost primal wailing, "My head! Oh, my head! Help me, Mummy! Ooooohh noooooooo!" A horrible squeal and then more violent vomiting.

I had never seen anything like it. It was worse than before, and I desperately tried to stay composed. Something truly awful and *wrong* was happening. It was as though evil had taken over my tiny child's body. Mercilessly, the violent spasms continued.

Images of *The Exorcist* ridiculously burst into my mind as I fought to take control of the frightening scene. I *had* to get the other kids out. I told

George to go and wait in our bedroom—I'd be right there. I asked Jess to get me some warm water and a towel, then join her brother.

The vomiting continued. How could so much come from such a tiny body?

Ollie's face looked different.

On high alert, I couldn't show my fear. Protecting him from it, I maintained a calm demeanor.

As the vomiting subsided, Ollie laid his head on my lap, crying softly. His face was full of pain, and he was unable to speak, his little body spent of energy.

Stroking and wiping him clean, I noticed for the first time something strange. His left eye looked odd, like it wasn't straight or something, like it had *moved*. "Sweetie, baby, does your head still hurt?" It was a stupid question, but I asked it anyway.

He nodded. He looked sad, exhausted, scared. Thankfully he was asleep almost immediately.

He would sleep ten straight hours.

⁓⌇⁓

Ollie's episode had finished, yet it was just the beginning of traumatic events to come. Symptoms of what was secretly growing inside my child were now presenting themselves in force, and I returned to the doctor, who still felt it was unnecessary to get an MRI. He once again reassured me there was nothing serious to worry about, and I stupidly believed him. I trusted him.

When I pointed out that Ollie's left eye seemed to have moved slightly, the doctor said lazy eyes were common in kids and they grew out of them. He suggested I take him to an eye doctor.

Yet my uneasiness was now permanent, and I wanted a second opinion.

I called Pete and told him what had happened, what the doctor had said, and that I was nervous something was truly wrong with our son. It was difficult to explain the enormity of the situation when he was so far away and had yet to witness the true impact of what was happening. The last time he'd visited home, Ollie had gotten a headache, yet nothing else had occurred: no screaming pain, violent vomiting, or unusual lethargy. With the information he had, Pete was not as concerned as I was, and he leaned toward accepting the advice of our doctor.

It was almost as though this thing was mocking us, waiting with its evil: *It's okay. Your baby's okay. I'm just playing with you guys. Ha-ha! You can't see me. Don't worry, be happy.* It smirked at us as we silently and fearlessly stood by while it intruded and took up residence inside our child and began making cruel plans.

Finally, however, my persistence for a second opinion paid off, and Pete arranged a consultation with a pediatrician in London. We explained this to our children, who obviously knew Ollie had been sick a lot lately. During our upcoming trip, we would visit a special doctor who could help Ollie, and then we would continue with our fun plans.

Not overly concerned, the kids just nodded and said, "Okay," before quickly moving on to the excitement of our vacation.

CHAPTER 2
Journey into the Unknown

The kids bounced in anticipation as we made our way to the airport for the long flight to England. Meanwhile I prayed Ollie would be okay for eight hours in the pressure-filled cabin.

Thankfully, my prayers were answered. While I enjoyed the in-flight movie and chatted with fellow passengers, the kids enjoyed their coloring books, games, and activities and had a wonderful time. I hoped this was a good sign.

After Pete picked us up from the airport, we headed to his apartment with three tired yet excited children. The kids were super happy to be with their dad, and with a smile I watched them playing.

Sharing a glass of wine with Pete as I prepared

dinner, I noticed with hope that it felt good to be with him again. He always was so fun to be with, and I giggled at his antics with the kids. It was going to be a lovely evening together.

Yet I couldn't put out of my mind the following day's appointment with the pediatrician. I wished the sense of foreboding would go away.

We rose early, fed the kids, and made our way to the Docklands Light Railway to ride to town. Ollie insisted on travelling in the very first carriage so he could pretend to be the driver steering the train. This surprised none of us, and we dutifully obliged.

We arrived at our destination right on time. The practice in the grand, four-story Victorian house on Harley Street was friendly, inviting, and full of toys. Standing by a huge fireplace was a worn wooden rocking horse with a handsome mane. Ollie stared at it longingly.

Meanwhile, Jessica and George sat on a red couch tossing cushions at one another.

"Kids, please," I said sternly, frowning.

Pete stood to greet the receptionist. "Hello. We've got an appointment with Dr. Harding. Oliver Tibbles, 11:30."

"He'll be right with you," the receptionist responded, smiling, though her eyes were fixed on Ollie.

The moment Dr. Harding saw Ollie, I knew we were in for bad news. Something in his kind eyes told me, *Prepare yourself; this child is in danger.*

The consultation went smoothly. This kind man had the Midas touch, and Ollie laughed throughout the consultation.

"Follow your eyes as far as the train will go, Ollie. Choo-choo!" Dr. Harding held up a finger, moving it from left to right.

Giggling, Ollie obliged.

When the exam was over, Ollie returned to the waiting room and Pete and I waited in the doctor's office. I shifted in my seat, nervously looking at Pete, who seemed perfectly calm. The silence was deafening. I tried to will my racing heart to calm down so I could hear what the doctor would say.

"I'm going to be honest with you, Mr. and Mrs. Tibbles. We are definitely going to find something. Your son's skull circumference and the turning of his left eye in a relatively short period of time give me great cause for concern. I've also detected some pressure. The optic nerve, directly behind his eye, is swollen. That, along with the symptoms Oliver has displayed, is worrisome. I'm arranging for Oliver to be seen immediately for an MRI scan of his brain at Great Ormond Street Hospital. Then I want you to come back here with the results so that we can see what we're up against and help your son."

Pete reached for my hand.

I squeezed his. *Oh God, oh no. Oh God, please.* Thoughts of the worst kind crashed into each other. *Don't let this be happening. Let him be okay. Please, please God.* I fought back tears.

We gathered the kids and jumped into a black cab. The kids, who thought we were merely on an adventure, chatted boisterously. We saw no point in causing any worry until we ourselves knew.

Pete and I decided it would be best if I stayed with Ollie and he took Jess and George for a long walk.

~~~

Upon entering the MRI unit, I filled out paperwork while the radiologist explained what the scan would be: basically a cellular photograph of the brain.

"The patient has to remain completely still. If he moves, we'll have to do the pictures all over again."

"What? For how long?"

"Oh, about an hour. Maybe longer if he moves. And FYI, it's noisy."

"Oh, is it? I was going to read him a story

26

while it was being done."

The radiologist gave me a wry smile. "Well, you can try, but it might prove a little difficult."

We were led to a large, sparse room with a machine that looked like a massive tunnel with a long stretcher type of bed in the middle of it. The bed was covered in starchy sheets and had straps dangling on each side, the kind you'd see in an asylum. I glanced at Ollie curled up in his buggy, his wide-eyed gaze darting from the machine to me.

I hoped he wouldn't be scared. The tunnel was huge. I could fit him and his buggy right inside of it.

A computerized key pad flashed zero near the machine. Behind large glass windows and a wide heavy door, somber technicians stared at luminous screens. Barely moving, they looked spookily like identical mannequins in white coats.

Suddenly, one of them sprang to life, speaking loudly through a microphone: "Can you hear me okay, Mrs. Tibbles?"

Nodding, I gave a thumbs-up. Then I lifted Ollie out of his buggy, set him on the table, and took off his shoes. His little legs dangled over the edge, so high he'd need help getting down. The headrest was far too big, so I rolled up some towels nearby to secure his head properly.

"Why do I have to do this, Mummy?" Ollie

asked for the millionth time, somewhat nervously.

I explained again. "The kind doctor with the rocking horse wants to take a picture inside your head. He's worried too, sweetie, about those nasty headaches and is going to help us make them go away. But first we need these pictures, okay?"

"Oh, all right then," he said, yawning. "Will you read me a story, Mummy? *The Three Little Pigs*? I like that one." He'd seen the book on a table nearby as we'd entered.

"Of course I will," I said and reminded Ollie he'd have to keep still and not move a muscle.

The radiologist came in with extra blankets and strapped him in tightly.

"Like a bug in a rug," I said, smiling.

"I'm a sandwich!"

"Yes you are, my darling," I responded, laughing. "Now you keep still." As he smiled, I prayed he would be able to. I pulled up a chair to read to him and opened the book.

Then the machine woke up. A few short definitive clicks, then bang, bang, bang! Click, click, click! Bang, bang, bang!

"Bloody hell," I mouthed to myself. "This is utterly ridiculous." I could not believe the incredible noise!

Then a continuous baaaaamm, baaaaamm!

I looked at the page, then at Ollie, then yelled at the top of my voice, "Once upon a time! There were three little pigs!" I burst out laughing. It was quite a comical situation indeed. "Can you hear me, sweetie?"

Ollie nodded.

"Oh, okay! Don't move. Good boy!" Somehow I managed to read the whole story, and my darling child stayed perfectly still. Just five years old, and not an inch did he move.

～◦◦◦～

Afterward, Pete, Jess, and George met up with us again, and we headed back to Dr. Harding's office with the MRIs.

In the waiting room, Ollie rode the rocking horse while his bored big siblings shouted, "Can we go now?"

I welcomed the normalcy.

It was short-lived. While the kids continued to be bored in the waiting area, we were led into the office and seated.

That's when the statement I never thought I would hear sprang forth.

"Your son has a brain tumor."

"What?" I heard but didn't want to hear.

"It needs to be removed. I'm going to make

some calls and have Oliver admitted immediately. His condition is serious, I'm afraid. His life is in danger."

The words hung in the air, and I gasped from the impact of them. I couldn't quite believe what was being said.

Yet somehow I knew and had known for a while—and I had done nothing. My baby was suffering, and I had lingered. Why? I should have taken him back to our doctor weeks before and demanded an MRI. How could I have been so ignorant? Why had I not listened to what the voice was telling me?

I looked at Pete, whose eyes were full of tears, and felt my own eyes stinging.

Our own doctor had failed to notice key signs of a pediatric brain tumor and had misdiagnosed our child.

Everything was happening so fast. I had so many questions, yet there was no time to ask.

The doctor gave us a letter of referral to Dr. Haywood, neurosurgeon at Great Ormond Street Hospital. In large letters, it said, Urgent Medical Intervention.

In a haze, we silently made our way to the hospital.

Strangely, even the kids were quiet.

Upon arriving, we made our way to the neuro-surgical unit waiting area.

The kids soon found the playroom where volunteers would keep an eye on them while Pete and I met with the surgeon.

Dr. Haywood was kind and to the point. A large tumor on Ollie's brain stem needed to be removed immediately or he would be dead in a matter of days or weeks.

Speechless, we listened.

He would perform a biopsy to determine whether the tumor was benign or malignant. It would be a week before we knew.

The date was March 27, 2002, and Ollie's surgery was planned a few days from then.

Why? I kept asking myself. *Why did this have to happen to my child? He's innocent. Why him? What did I do wrong?*

Dr. Haywood explained that in rare cases, a certain type of cancer dropped to the spine. As a matter of caution, anytime tumors were found in the brain, spinal MRIs were taken as well. Ollie was scheduled for one the next day.

Numbly, we nodded. It all seemed too much. Thoughts swirling, we didn't have the energy to sort through the chaos.

The first medication was prescribed to Ollie, a steroid called Dexamethasone that helps to reduce swelling and alleviate pressure. Hopefully it would help combat some of his horrendous symptoms.

When we left the room to collect the kids, a nurse asked us if we needed some time.

We both nodded.

Pete and I walked down the hospital corridor holding hands, the enormity of what we had just been told smashing into us and breaking us down. For Pete, the floodgates opened. This big, strong, six-foot-tall man let go of my hand and walked alone down the long hallway, sobbing uncontrollably, oblivious to those walking past with sympathetic looks.

I couldn't comfort him. He didn't want me to, and that was okay. I watched him grieve his helplessness and offered a silent prayer for his strength—and my own. I didn't want the kids to see us both in such a state.

After about half an hour, we made our way back to Dr. Harding's office, where one of the nurses guided us to a private bathroom where we could freshen up before collecting the kids from the playroom, where according to the nurse, they were having a grand ol' time.

As we cleaned up, we briefly discussed our plan to tell Ollie and the kids once we got home. It all seemed so surreal. What the heck was I going to say?

Suddenly it dawned on me that I had to make some phone calls. Our families were oblivious to what was happening. The burden weighed heavily on my shoulders.

Before making that first call, I bought some coffee and cigarettes, both strangely comforting. I found a designated area overlooking a small courtyard where fellow smokers spoke on cell phones, many in tears. Finding a spot, I sat among my newfound comrades.

So this was where everyone came for bad news. Tears and cigarettes. *Just like the movies,* I idiotically thought.

My glances caught the attention of a woman leaning against a railing. Eyes puffy, she half smiled and nodded.

I nodded back. With cigarette in hand, I took a deep breath, picked up the phone, and started dialing.

How do you tell your loved ones your child has a brain tumor? That he'll be in surgery in a couple of days? That he might die?

Human nature is to protect the ones we love. How could I tell my mum in a way that would not hurt so much?

There was no good way. I couldn't candy coat

it or hide the shocking tragedy of it.

Every time I had to repeat what was happening, the hurt was palpable. People could not believe it. I had to take breaks. I was a raging mess.

While I was on one side of the courtyard talking to my family, Pete was on the other talking to his. It seemed weird yet also *right*. Without explanation, we seemed to sense the energy of tragedy, how it sucked *everything* out of us. We dealt with two sets of calls, two sets of shocked families, two sets of confusion and pain. It was simply *unbearable*, though we supported each other.

Exhausted and weepy from the calls, we cleaned up a second time and went to pick up our children from the playroom. Oblivious to it all, they had enjoyed the two hours of play and proudly showed us their paintings. It took all I had to not burst.

It felt good to finally be out of the hospital. On the way to Pete's apartment, we stopped by Starbucks. The treat of chocolate cake for the kids gave us a welcome moment of normalcy in the face of an uncertain future.

On a high dose of steroids, Ollie eventually found relief from the episodes. It was such a joy to see our

OLLIE TIBBLES: THE BOY WHO BECAME A TRAIN

little boy smile again. Along with relief, the steroids gave Ollie a huge appetite. He would eat whatever he fancied until his full tummy looked like a huge oval balloon. We joked that he had a potbelly bigger than his dad's, which caused much hilarity.

It was one evening while we were seated for dinner and Ollie was on his third helping that we broached the subject of his tumor. Pete began by chatting about the fact that Ollie had been really sick recently and we were trying to find out what the problem was. "And as you know, we had some MRIs taken of Ollie's brain, which, as Mum explained, are like photographs of inside his head."

I looked at Ollie. "Sweetie, they did find something. It's called a brain tumor, and that's what's giving you the bad headaches and sickness."

Jess and George listened intently.

"What's a brain tumor?" Ollie asked, looking at us with wide innocent eyes. Chocolate pudding coated his lovely lips.

The wonder of children is their innocence and their ability to absorb information at face value. Whenever our children had asked us questions on any subject matter, we'd replied with the truth, and this would be no different. At the same time, we did not want our children to be frightened unnecessarily. I explained carefully yet lightheartedly, as if we were discussing how to bake a cake. It was unreal.

"How did it get there?" George said.

"Yeah, how, Mummy?" Ollie said. "Can we get it out?"

I carried on. "Well, right now they still don't know how children get brain tumors. It's just something that happens to some kids and not to others. The doctors are trying to find out. They think it might be a nasty germ you might get from outside in the air, or it might be something some kids are born with. We really don't know, but we can get it out and then you'll feel so much better. As you know, we have some medicine for you now, which is already helping, isn't it?"

Ollie nodded, smiling, then added, "I don't like the bad sickness, Mummy." He looked up at me through his long, dark, curly eyelashes.

"I know you don't, sweetie. We're going to take care of you, baby. I promise. Everything's going to be just fine." I stroked his head and silently prayed it would be.

The spine MRI results were in.

"I'm sorry to have to tell you this, but Oliver

does have tumors present in his spine." As usual, our kind, rather grim-faced Dr. Haywood told us straight.

Pete and I sat rigidly in our seats, minds reeling at yet more bad news.

"As you know, we have Oliver scheduled for surgery in a couple of days to remove the tumor. However, I will not be as aggressive, because we have lesions present in the spine, which present a risk of paralysis. I'll get out as much as I can, but chances are that some will remain."

My heart was racing.

"Does this mean the tumor is malignant?" Pete said. "Does Ollie have cancer?"

"Can you take out the tumor in his spine?" I said.

Quietly, Dr. Haywood answered. "I'm afraid the chances of this tumor being malignant are high, but of course we won't know for sure until the biopsy is done."

We were being bombarded with one thing after another. At some point, I reached for Pete's hand.

He looked broken, bewildered.

My mind momentarily wandered to Ollie, who was with a hospital volunteer in the playroom. The room itself was brightly colored with Winnie the Pooh pictures accompanied by many other children favorites from Disney, Nickelodeon, and, of course, Thomas the Tank Engine,

Ollie's favorite. Also displayed were many children's drawings: little handprints, cute stickmen with huge beaming faces, and nurses of all shapes and sizes with the words *I love you* and *Thank you*. Laughter, music, and nursery rhymes always drifted out to the hallway. I imagined him in the room making his way around invisible tracks on his knees, pushing his trains, changing the switches, and choo-chooing loudly.

Fighting back tears, I gulped and brought my mind back to the meeting, though I wanted to run away. I had heard enough. I needed fresh air. I wanted a cigarette. I fought to keep my feelings, including the anger, at bay, but I was losing it.

CHAPTER 3
Riding into Battle

We made plans for Jess and George to stay with relatives during Ollie's surgery and recovery. We would not be returning to the United States and our home in Downers Grove, Illinois, for at least two to three months.

When we notified our employers of our situation, they were saddened and offered us their support. I took leave from my job at the YMCA, where I was the fitness coordinator, so I could care for Ollie and our other children full-time. Once back in the States, Pete would return to work as soon as he was able, which was tough for him because he wanted to be with his son during this difficult time. However, bills had to be paid and he knew he had no choice.

During our time in London, our families were incredibly supportive, pulling out the stops to help. I don't know how we would have survived without them. Our emotions were raw, and it felt good to be able to cry openly, to scream at the unfairness of it all without trying to hide or compose ourselves. We gained strength from their love and also from others when floods of cards, e-mails, and packages started arriving at the hospital from our friends and coworkers back in the US. It was overwhelming yet fantastic, and eventually these gifts would adorn Ollie's room on Parrot Ward, the neurological unit where he would recover following surgery.

It was Pete who suggested I talk to Ollie about his upcoming surgery, and I was grateful. I wanted it to be me. When a child is sick, it is always Mummy they want. I knew it would be difficult to make him fully understand the impact of surgery, but he was a smart kid and I would be honest right from the start. I would tell him he may be hurting when he woke but the doctors had strong medicine that would take away the pain. I would tell him he would have to sleep in the hospital but one of us would always be by his side. I would tell him he would have bandages around his head and tubes on his body. I would tell him everything.

I did tell him all of this, and I also told him the kids got better and all went home eventually. And I told him how much I loved him and that he was my special, brave soldier.

He asked lots of questions.

One of great importance was, "Will I eat breakfast

and dinner there on a tray?"

I laughed. "Of course. You'll be waited on hand and foot, like a king."

He sat up in his chair, looking pompous.

I played along and bowed before him. "Your Majesty."

Giggling, he slapped my hand. "Mummy, you're silly."

"They give you a menu, Ollie, just like they do in the restaurants."

His eyes were wide. "Wow." He paused. "What if they don't have what I want?"

I chuckled and, cupping his cute face in my hands, I kissed his eyelids and his nose before giving him a big squeeze. "You're such a funny little boy. Don't worry. We'll make sure you get what you want, you cheeky monkey."

Jess and George would also have questions. They understood their brother was really sick and were scared for him. They wanted to know if he would be in pain, and Pete and I reassured them that the strong medicine would help Ollie.

The day of surgery was upon us. Dressed in his underpants and blue teddy bear hospital gown and matching socks, Ollie was ready. His thoughts were of food, given that he was nil by mouth prior to surgery.

We told him he could eat after his operation and even offered up the all-you-can-eat card, yet still he grumbled.

Our wait over, the hospital transport team arrived to take Ollie to the surgical preparation area.

With thoughts of his empty tummy gone, Ollie once again asked what was happening and where were we going.

"Well," I explained, "these nice men are going to take us to the special room where you will be having a lovely long sleep so that they can take that nasty tumor out of your head. Remember, Ollie? Remember what Daddy and I were saying about the strong medicine that makes you fall asleep quickly?"

He nodded and nervously played with his comfort item of choice, "Ticky."

Each of our children had been attached to a special item early in life. Our firstborn, Jessica, had her beloved crib blanket, soft with a silk edge, which she held to her face and caressed as she sucked her thumb. George's was an old pair of pajama bottoms he only needed at bedtime. I learned of our Ollie's quite by accident. He had a favorite Thomas the Tank Engine vest, and whenever he wore it, I noticed he would frequently reach his hand down the back of it.

Curious, I asked him what he was doing.

"I'm playing with Ticky, silly!" He turned around to show me a long, silky washing label sticking up out of the vest.

"This is Ticky?" I touched the label. "And you play with him?"

Ollie spun around and looked at me as though I had two heads. "Of course. Hello!" He rolled his eyes. "He's the softest Ticky there is!"

I tried not to laugh. "Ollie, you know that vest is getting a little too small for you, and it must be hard playing with Ticky with your arm stuck over your head, so how about we take the vest off and then you can have Ticky with you all the time?"

Of course, he thought this was a splendid idea. With a huge grin, he whipped off his vest, hugged Ticky, and gave me a lovely, sloppy kiss.

Ticky would become a constant source of comfort to our child as our journey continued.

Ollie clung to Ticky and Pete and I held each of his hands as the transport team wheeled him toward the elevator.

Nurses shouted cheerfully, "Good luck," and "See you soon, Ollie. We'll have some chocolate ice cream waiting for you when you get back."

Ollie gave them a silly smile and poked out his tongue.

Entering the surgical preparation unit, we met the anesthesiologist, who shook our hands and smiled broadly. "Well, hello there, Oliver—or is it Ollie?"

Ollie, obviously anxious and not wanting to be there at all, turned his head away. The fear of the unknown and the sight of this towering stranger dressed in surgical uniform, mask, and plastic gloves must have appeared to be something out of a scary story.

The hospital smell was hygiene-gone-haywire, so strong we could feel it in our nostrils, taste it in our throats.

Ollie glanced all around, taking in everything: the stretchers with straps on the other side of the room, the blinking and beeping monitors, the metal poles with bags of fluid hanging down, and the table set up with frightening instruments. With his gaze on that table, as if woken from a nightmare, Ollie started to scream.

Pete and I tried to calm him, to no avail.

"Quick," I yelled. "Please. Let's get started now."

Suddenly I wished I hadn't sounded so panic-stricken. It only made it worse for our inconsolably terrified son. While a nurse put a mask over his face, Pete and I held him down.

Almost without Ollie's realizing it, the anesthesiologist inserted the needle and we waited for sleep to come to our son. Tears rolled slowly down his cheeks as his cries grew silent, his body limp while the drug took effect.

We stroked our child, kissing him and telling him, "Go bye-byes, baby. Go sleepies. We love you. We'll see you soon."

Ollie's eyelids fluttered, his beautiful lashes wet from tears, and then they closed.

He was out, and the medical staff could begin their work.

Armed with a pager, we left the hospital traumatized. Perhaps the crisp fresh air would clear our minds.

With several long hours ahead, we had an opportunity to talk about the way forward and share our thoughts. Or not. Maybe having time to think was all we needed.

Walking aimlessly through the streets of London, I took in the scene—suits rushing to The Tube, mothers with strollers, couples hand in hand, noisy traffic heading who knows where—and I envied the simple state of being normal when everything in our world was so *not*.

The pager went off, bringing me back to my new, unknown world.

Returning to the intensive care unit, we heard a nurse talking loudly, almost shouting, "All right now, Oliver! Try not to move. Keep still, Oliver. Try to keep still!"

Ollie wailed, "Muuuummmmyy! I want my muuummmmy!" Louder: "Get off!" His words were slurred, slow with long pauses, and I could tell this was making him all the angrier. "Noooo, noooo, noooo!"

Nurses held him down trying to stop him from ripping out the lines and tubes from his arms, hands, and feet. It was a frantic, horrible scene.

We rushed to his side, and I did a quick once-over: his head was swathed in bandages; lines were connected to monitors registering heart rate, blood pressure, respiration, oxygen levels; metal poles held numerous bags. Ticky was inside a bag at the end of his bed along with his gown and soiled underpants.

Fighting back tears, I took Ollie's hand and put Ticky in it. "Here you go, baby. Here's Ticky, and Mummy's right here. Daddy too. We love you. You're such a brave boy."

Pete, who was trying to stay composed, also reassured our son.

However, Ollie was having none of it. If anything, our presence seemed to make things worse, and Ollie wailed louder.

This was a violent awakening for a five-year-old: the tremendous pain, the feeling of no control, the shocking fearful question of why he felt this way.

I felt I had betrayed him. I just *knew* what he was thinking: *You never told me it was going to be like this. You lied to me, Mummy.* I was supposed to be the protector, and I had failed. It was the worst feeling of my life.

Thankfully, morphine released our son from his waking nightmare, and he drifted into a deep and peaceful sleep.

While Ollie slept, a Sister briefed us on Ollie's condition. He was doing well, the operation had been a success, and doctors and staff were happy. Dr. Haywood would visit in the morning to speak to us in more detail about the procedure, Ollie's recovery, and what we could expect as the days went by.

Smiling kindly, she suggested that we get some sleep.

This presented a problem Pete and I hadn't had time to consider. Only one parent was allowed to sleep at the bedside. Those were the rules. Of course it made perfect sense. We should go home and sleep. We needed the rest in order to get through the next day, but I didn't care about the rules or that they made sense. I wanted to be with my son, and so did Pete.

Emotionally and irrationally I tried to bargain with the Sister and doctors alike, with my husband on the sidelines trying to calm me. I knew it was a no-win situation, yet I childishly insisted that both of us would stay until finally, like many parents before me, I accepted the sensibility of the rule and reluctantly gave in.

Still, I did not want to go home. How could I sleep anyway?

Standing on either side of Ollie's bed, Pete and I argued over who should stay the first night. I wanted to be with Ollie every minute of the day, and I hated the idea of sharing that with anyone, even his father. The Sister suggested we both leave for the evening, explaining that following such a procedure the children slept for hours. Her easygoing manner was calming, as if Ollie had merely had a tooth, instead of a brain tumor, removed.

We looked at each other, accepting the suggestion. Then we looked at Ollie, savoring the moment. Stroking his hand, making sure Ticky was tucked safely inside, we gently kissed him good-bye until the morning.

Arriving at Pete's apartment, I suddenly felt a pang of guilt. We hadn't spoken to Jess or George in almost two days. I called my sister Karen, who was caring for them at her home, and briefed her on the day. Then I spoke with Jess and George, who were having a marvelous time. I told them Ollie was doing fine, the operation was a success, and he was sleeping. Then I changed the subject, telling them I missed them and asking them about their plans with Aunty Karen.

They told me excitedly that they would be visiting a farm next door and feeding the new spring lambs. They would also be seeing my mum, whom they had affectionately nicknamed Cranky Grandma because she liked to leave her false teeth out and whistled when she talked. My mum, who lived just around the corner from my sister, seemed to relish the pet name assigned her.

Pete also spoke with the kids and reminded them to take lots of pictures and told them we'd call again the next evening.

I was relieved and happy that they were being so well cared for and we were able to totally focus on Ollie and prepare ourselves for the next step.

It was well into the afternoon before Ollie finally woke. When he did, he was not the Ollie we'd known.

The doctors had told us what to expect: extreme mood swings, depression, anger, confusion, and frustration. He was certainly experiencing all of these, yet we were unprepared for the severity.

Ollie had gone into surgery, and a different child had come out. He was changed. Even though he would eventually recover from the surgery and his body would heal from the wounds inflicted, he was not the same. His persona, his soul, his being was different. When they opened up our child's skull and removed the evil within, something else was taken: a piece of our son that all the medicine in the world could not replace. His innocence.

Pete and I cared for our son as he struggled daily with what you and I take for granted: walking, talking, eating, laughing, and just being.

I pushed aside my feelings of sadness for the child I felt we had lost and began to embrace the Ollie I had not known: the part of our child that was hidden deep within and was called upon in an emergency for his survival. It was a side of him that had been asleep and, for most children, remains so. It began to emerge slowly yet was strong in its dignity and grace, and I found myself falling in love with Ollie all over again.

I no longer mourned our lost child, for he had

found his secret weapon that he would call upon time and again to protect those he loved and, in the process, regain some of his lost innocence. I wanted to know this newfound comrade, this spirit that could not be broken, this silent strength. An invisible passenger called courage had joined us on our journey.

Our child had awoken from his surgery unable to speak coherently, eat, drink, control his bladder and bowels, or walk. With his fine motor skills affected, he could no longer color in his favorite Thomas books or write his name. He had to start from scratch with everything. Yet he would do all these things again, and I loved him more than ever as I watched him overcome every obstacle.

Fiercely independent, Ollie insisted on trying to do everything himself. For example, he was *not* going to use the bedpan. He would walk to the bathroom, dragging the IV pole with him, only to fall and painfully struggle to stand again. "I can do it by myself!" he'd scream. If we tried to help him, with a rageful look upon his face, he would yell, "Go away!"

Ollie's mood swings were unpredictable. He was happy one day, incredibly sad the next. A terrible depression would blanket his whole body, and he looked as if he were sinking, disappearing into a black void. With his head bowed and shoulders down, he was enveloped in an unreal darkness, the tears pouring down his cheeks. He would look up at me through his soaked lashes and ask, "Why, Mummy? Why am I so sad? I'm so sad, so sad." Shaking his head, he would reach for me and want to be held.

I would climb on the bed and hold him close, caressing my beautiful, sorrowful child. With soothing words and murmurs, I comforted him the way only a mother can.

As Ollie fought his battles, Pete and I fought our own. We had not forgotten about the biopsy. However, without words, we put the impending news to the back of our minds. We were learning pretty fast that whatever energy we did have was best saved, and it seemed pointless to dwell on bad news.

Six days after Ollie's surgery, we met with Dr. Haywood and his team.

"I'm sorry," Dr. Haywood began. "Oliver has cancer."

What? my mind screamed.

"The type of tumor that Oliver has is highly malignant," he continued. "Extremely aggressive. It's called medulloblastoma. Let me spell it for you. M-E-D-U-L-L-O-B-L-A-S-T-O-M-A. As you are aware, he does have lesions present in the spine, and we could not remove five percent of the brain tumor. This type of cancer . . ."

I was trembling. I was aware as he spoke that I was losing control. From deep within, a savage fury was about to explode. My trembles turned into violent shaking. Sweat oozed from my every pore. *No. This cannot be. Not my baby. Please, God, no!*

Unable to sit, I stood and paced the room, clinging to the doctor's every word but not believing this was actually happening to Ollie, to us, to me.

" . . . and this type of cancer," he went on, "will by its nature spread aggressively in a relatively short time, so it is of the utmost importance that we start his treatment as soon as possible. He will be diagnosed level four, high risk."

Through my manic fog, I vaguely heard Pete ask about statistics.

Twelve percent survival was the response, with *cure* cruelly left out.

The words floated away, yet the acute impact of what they meant hit me like a tsunami.

My mouth was dry. I felt sick. My heart was smashing against my chest. An unrecognizable force was rising inside, taking me away from myself. Out of nowhere, my body and soul came together in defense of my child. With a brutal surge, the uncontrollable emotions won, and a sound like no other filled the room. I was unaware that it was my own voice.

While my husband sat quietly weeping, I raged a private war, and no one stopped me. As looks of pity spread across the faces of Dr. Haywood and his team, I fought my demons alone: demons of desperation, helplessness, and terrifying pain, as if someone had ripped my child from my womb while I lay bleeding with my guts spread grotesquely across an empty belly. My fury, which up till now I had confined, broke loose as evil spewed from my mouth like a maggot-infested piece of flesh. I chewed it willingly, savoring each foul bite before I spat it out viciously. The wrath of pain continued to slither across my skin and into my pores like a monstrous serpent as its grip tightened, squeezing out of me vile filth as I venomously challenged God in a room where no one raised an eyebrow.

"Noooo! How the fuck could you? How fucking *dare you*? *Why*? Not my son. Not my Ollie! He's just a baby. He's done nothing wrong! What did I do?" My stomach contorted with violent sobs as I sat rocking on the floor. "I'm sorry! I'll do anything. He's innocent. I'm sorry. For fuck's sake, please. No. *No*," I begged a deaf ear.

God was out. The door was shut and a Do Not Disturb sign was posted.

I was dead inside. Worse, I was undead, condemned to walk alongside my son the eternity of his suffering and eventual death. With futility, I pleaded to the eyes in the room, my nose snotty, dripping down my chin and onto the floor, the racks of sobs subsiding as I waited for their response.

None came.

Howling screams erupted from my mouth. My condemnation was real. The nightmare was real. I felt my body disintegrate as I lay crumpled on the floor like a worthless old sack, the kind that you kick to the corner, the kind that is rough, brittle, and full of holes.

Only when I punched the walls, knuckles bleeding, did my husband rise from his chair. Wiping away his own tears, he took hold of me.

With arms flailing, I continued to punch at the air, at him, at God, before I collapsed into his chest, into a black nothingness.

I do not recollect how much time had passed. I only know that I was spent.

Now I was ready for the fight of my life.

Ollie would undergo sixty-eight weeks of therapy, including high-dose radiation and chemotherapy. Already the remaining tumor was growing along with the lesions in his spine. In order for him to have a longer life expectancy and better chance at survival, treatment was to begin as soon as possible. Time was not on our side, and the sense of urgency grew. Even though four weeks had passed since surgery, Ollie was still in recovery phase and not well enough for the impact of therapy. Neither was he fit to travel.

In order to save precious time, we discussed the option of treatment in London. However, several issues arose which helped make our decision. We had family members who lived in different parts of the

United Kingdom and were unable to help on a long-term basis. Our other children needed to return to school. Pete's apartment was not set up for a family of five. Our home and jobs were in the United States. We had friends in our Illinois neighborhood lining up to offer assistance in the care of our son.

Finally, a major factor in our decision was Dr. Haywood's recommendation of Dr. Stewart Goldman, a man at the forefront of pediatric brain tumor research, a brilliant scientist based at Children's Memorial Hospital in Chicago. Dr. Stew, as his patients and colleagues affectionately called him, would soon change our lives.

I had heard about Children's Memorial Hospital. In fact, it was located only a few miles from our home. The previous year, I had listened to Eric and Kathy on 101.9 The Mix, Chicago's top radio station, during the annual fund-raiser for Children's Memorial. While patients and families had shared their stories, I'd been deeply affected, particularly by those who were patients on the oncology unit. I'd found myself calling the radio station to make a donation.

What an ironic, cruel twist of fate that now we too would be joining those families.

Our decision was made, and in the following two months of Ollie's recovery at Great Ormond Street, preparations were being made for our return to the States and our consultation with Dr. Goldman.

Ollie continued to progress in his surgical recovery, and one morning not long before we were due to leave London, there was palpable excitement on the ward. Passing the nurses' station to get Ollie some juice from the kitchen, I saw some of the girls brushing their hair and putting on lipstick. Even the male nurses were preening.

I didn't pay much attention, but I was curious. I took Ollie his juice and drank my tea while he watched a *Thomas the Tank Engine* video. I would check out the commotion once I'd had my tea.

Our overnight nurse, Nicole, rushed in with a cheery smile. Breathless and wide-eyed, she put her finger to her mouth. "Oh my God, we have celebrities visiting the ward. They're going to be here in five minutes."

"What?" I said in disbelief. "Are you sure? Who is it?"

Ollie, transfixed with his Thomas video, kept eating his Coco Pops.

"I don't know," Nicole said. "They won't tell us, but I do know that Geri Halliwell from Spice Girls and George Michael visit this unit often."

This I had to see.

Everyone who was able to walk was ushered into the children's playroom while the more seriously ill children remained in their beds and were brought

56

into the main unit. As a level four patient, Ollie fell into the latter category, so I wheeled him into the jam-packed room. Unhappy about being taken away from his video, he immediately sulked.

I must admit I felt pretty rotten for him, but I just had to see who this celebrity was. The Sister told us it would be a few more minutes and there would be two celebrities visiting the ward. Apparently these two came often, in secret, not wanting any publicity.

"Here they come," an excited Nicole shouted.

I could hardly believe my eyes when Madonna and Guy Ritchie walked in. Madonna held teddy bears, and Guy Ritchie cut a dashing figure all dressed in black.

Nicole positively drooled.

For a few seconds, I forgot where I was and imme-diately felt ridiculous in my pajamas and huge Donald Duck slippers, my hair a mess. When you're in the hos-pital 24-7, the last thing on your mind is your appear-ance. I couldn't even remember if I'd put on deodor-ant. I prayed I had.

Madonna, Ms. Glamour personified, made her way around the room. Surprisingly petite, she wore virtually no makeup yet still looked every inch the su-perstar. Taking her time at each bed, she chatted with the kids and parents. A mother herself, she clearly gen-uinely cared and felt the need to offer some support and help in some way.

As they made their way around the room, I noticed

Ollie was anxious. The noisy chitchat was getting to him, and I sensed his need to be alone.

Suddenly I felt guilty and was about to move him out when Madonna approached the bed.

She smiled, said hello to me, and gently asked Ollie's name as she handed him a teddy bear.

Ollie immediately threw the gift on the floor, frowned, and turned his back to her.

Not offended in the slightest, she looked at me with compassion.

I picked up the teddy bear and handed it back to her. "I'm sorry about that. Now, if you had been Thomas the Tank Engine, he just might have smiled."

She laughed and said she would remember that next time, and she wished us good luck.

All the way back to his room, Ollie grumbled.

However, I noticed a boost in the morale among the families on Parrot Ward, the neurological unit, and of the staff who worked in the stressful environment yet never complained.

It struck me how powerful stardom could be. Celebrities could create credence simply by their presence and effect massive change when they put their reputation toward a cause. I wished all of a sudden for fame so I, too, could make a difference. I wanted to unlock the chains of people who chose to close their eyes and ears because, like me, they didn't believe tragedy could ever happen to them. I faced the reality that at the end of the day, cancer didn't give a shit who you were, how much money you made, or how big your house was. I wanted to rally people around the cause of pediatric brain tumor research.

Yet I was not famous. I was a nobody in the eyes of the world. I was a mother with a sick child who simply wanted to be heard. Would anybody listen to me? Did anybody care?

Our last days at Great Ormond Street were tinged with sadness for me. We were leaving the wonderful staff and patients with whom we had formed close bonds.

Ollie, on the other hand, couldn't wait to leave. If he could have, he would've jumped and skipped his way out the front hospital doors. "I'm going home," he shouted as we wheeled past the nurses' station in the new, shiny, black buggy we'd gotten days earlier.

He was greeted with happy shouts of, "Hooray," and "Good luck, Ollie. We'll miss you!"

As we approached the exit doors of Parrot Ward at Great Ormond Street Hospital, I turned and took one last glance. There was Jo, twelve years old, who had been a patient on the ward for several months and whose room was directly opposite Ollie's. She had suffered horrific injuries in a traffic accident when she'd been catapulted from her parents' vehicle directly onto the highway and miraculously had not been hit by oncoming vehicles. She had almost died in the ambulance, had been in a coma for several weeks, and up until that day had spent her time in a wheelchair. Now she was walking slowly, unaided, to her room.

Smiling, I turned and exited the hospital with hope in my heart. Our flight was booked. Finally, we were going home.

CHAPTER 4
A Clown and a Magic Table

Back in the States, our friends in the neighborhood immediately came together to support us, no questions asked. Wanting to do something, anything, to ease our situation, they took turns taking care of Jess and George, cooked meals, ran errands, did laundry, and did whatever was needed. I counted my lucky stars to have such friends who welcomed us with open arms into the neighborhood. Toni and John Cesarz's children bonded closely with our own, and we would spend many weekend gatherings around the fire pit along with others we got to know over the years: the Whites, the Giuffres, the Zowodniaks, the Taylors, the Kennedys, the Haraps, the Swicks, the Khuns, the Hansons, the

Houks, the Huizingers, the Smiths, and others I barely knew but who offered their assistance regardless.

We needed the support. Despite the successful surgery, Ollie was not doing well. He was in great pain and unable to walk, and the angry sadness had returned to such a degree that I could almost feel his misery. I felt helpless.

On the day of our consultation with Dr. Stewart Goldman, neighbors watched Jess and George and Pete drove me and Ollie to Children's. I sat in the back stroking Ollie's cheek as he rested his head in my lap. He held my hand, squeezing it every so often.

At Children's, we reported to reception in the fourth-floor oncology unit, then sat on the pale-blue leather couches to wait.

Before I actually saw Stew, I heard him.

A man was singing somewhat out of tune.

Turning toward the happy-go-lucky voice, I saw this big, six-foot-plus man striding down the hallway, talking to the kids as he passed. "Hey, David, how ya doin'? Got any good booger jokes for me, buddy?" he asked a plump, bald boy riding his IV pole like a scooter toward the day hospital.

David laughed. "Sorry, Stew. Not today. I'll have some next week for ya."

To a young, wispy-haired girl, Stew purred,

"Hey, there's my girlfriend."

She positively blushed. "Oh, Stew."

Wearing a permanent grin and a Mickey Mouse Christmas tie even though it was May, Stew gave kids high-fives and strode onward like the Pied Piper. As he approached, I noticed Ollie's eyes widen as he gazed at the floor, where a trail of Tootsie Rolls flowed from Stew's trouser pockets. Delighted, kids eagerly swept them up. For that moment, I swear Ollie's pain was forgotten. I liked Stew immediately.

I looked at Pete, who was laughing, and smiled.

Pete nodded. "Yep, that's him all right."

We had heard rumors about this man who wore silly ties and told booger jokes. I wouldn't have been at all surprised if he'd been wearing goofy Ronald McDonald red shoes.

Holding out my hand, I approached Stew. "Dr. Goldman? Hi. Mrs. Tibbles. We're here with Oliver."

He beamed. "Hi. Nice to meet you finally." Shaking my hand and then Pete's, he added, "I'll be with you guys in five minutes. I have to finish up with a patient, and then we can chat."

Nodding, I sat and watched a girl, who was about ten years old, pass by. She was bald and walked with completely straight legs. I wondered why she had no flexion at the knees.

While we sat waiting for Stew, Ollie was becoming distressed. I gave him some pain relief, and he settled in his buggy, clutching Ticky as he tried to sleep.

At about 1:30 p.m., the oncology clinic was winding down and we were the only ones waiting in the main reception area with its cheerful mural-covered walls and comfy leather couches and chairs set neatly around the room.

At the large, square reception desk, three staff members took care of the endless paperwork, scheduled appointments, provided name tags, and prepped the clinic nurse, who recorded weight, height, and vitals before each child saw the doctor.

Over time, we would get to know this area well. Next to reception was the home of the volunteer group and family services for oncology/hematology, which provided practical and emotional support for families. Two doors down was the playroom staffed by volunteers with the same lively atmosphere we had experienced at Great Ormond Street.

At the end of the corridor was the day hospital, where patients went for blood and platelet transfusions. Chemotherapy was given here when an overnight stay wasn't required.

You knew you were in Stew's room when you saw the countless photographs of his patients proudly displayed on the walls. Some were old and faded. Others were more recent and shiny. There were so many smiling faces of babies, toddlers, children, and young teens. Most were boys about Ollie's age. In some, Stew was shown with the families, and surprisingly he did not look out of place but nestled right in. I stared at the children's faces, wondering how they were, what they were doing now—and whether they were still alive.

Stew was finally done, and after waving good-bye to his patient, he strolled over and pulled up a chair to sit with us. In front of the TV, Ollie sat in his buggy, uncomfortable and lying sideways, his legs pulled up and his back to us as he whimpered silently.

Stew glanced at Ollie as he shook hands with me and Pete. "I can see he's really unhappy," he said softly, "so I don't want to bother him today, okay?"

We both nodded, relieved.

Stew's big grin was replaced with a serious, gentle expression. "I've looked at Oliver's MRIs prior to his surgery and Dr. Haywood's case notes." Smiling, he added, "I'm sorry. Is it Oliver, or does he go by a different name?"

"He's Ollie," I said.

"Oh, okay, just wanted to make sure." He

looked at Ollie again and smiled. "I'm sure he's gonna tell me anyway, right?"

Pete and I grinned.

His serious look returned. "I'm sure you don't need me to tell you that Ollie's very sick. The first thing we need to do is get another MRI done to see where we are. It's been almost twelve weeks since his surgery, and I want to get treatment started right away."

"He's in so much pain," I said. "I don't know what to do."

"I can help with that. I'm gonna give you a prescription for some stronger medication that will make him more comfortable." He leaned closer, ensuring Ollie couldn't hear. "I'm gonna be honest with you guys. Ollie has a lot to go through, and it's gonna be tough. Yet I promise you this: I'll do everything and anything I can to make your boy well, to get him to smile, to be a kid again. He will feel better real soon. If you need to speak to me, you can call me day or night. If I'm not around, have them page me. Anytime. Just call me, okay? And we'll chat some more once we have the results of his MRIs."

Looking once more toward Ollie, who still had his back to us, he said, "I know he doesn't care for me right now, which is totally fine with me." He chuckled. "I wouldn't like me either if I was him."

Pete and I laughed.

"When Ollie finds out what's going to happen to him—and it's important that we're honest from the start—he will probably be angry. I don't want him to be mad at you guys, so when I see you after the MRIs, let me be the one to tell him. Let me be the one he gets aggravated with, okay? You guys will have enough to deal with."

His kind words lifted us, and I knew we had found the right doctor. His hope, delivered with such kindness, allowed me to believe that maybe, just maybe, Ollie would make it and not get lost in those statistics after all.

❧

With treatment about to begin, Stew briefed us again on Ollie's protocol of treatment, which would start as soon as his cast had been made. Because the tumor had dropped to his spine, Ollie would need an all-in-one cast in order for the radiation to be administered safely.

Once the cast was made, emergency radiation would continue every day for six weeks. Due to the mass of disease now present, Ollie would receive extremely high levels of radiation as well as a weekly dose of chemotherapy.

Monitoring would be vital. The toxicity would be so powerful it would render Ollie with virtually no immune system. Horrifying infections were commonplace: pneumonia, C. diff (diarrhea gone haywire with agonizing stomach cramps), fungal contamination of the blood, and meningitis, to name just a few.

I had many questions for Stew, one pressing topic being Ollie's hair. "Does it stop growing, come out in great chunks or patches, or what?"

His answer to all of these was, "Yes," and he said it would happen in a relatively short period of time.

I was worried about how this would affect Ollie and wondered how I could alleviate his concerns.

One day while a friend watched Ollie, I went to the salon. When I returned and entered the family room, I found Ollie playing with his trains.

"Mummy, you're *bald*," he squealed and promptly burst out laughing. Fascinated, he patted my scalp, stroked it, and then kissed it. He also asked why I'd done it.

"Well, sweetie, I just got really tired of having to do my hair every day, and now this is easy. I don't have to do anything. Besides, you know your mummy likes crazy hairstyles," I said, hugging him.

He lowered his head and looked up at me and then heavenward, a cheeky grin on his face as if he was thinking, *Oh, Lordy*. At the same time, his wise expression said, *I know why you did this*.

～⌒◯◦◯⌒～

Despite Stew's gracious offer to explain everything to Ollie, I wanted to tell him what was happening. As a mother, I felt I owed it to him.

That night, as I finished reading his bedtime story, I broached the subject. "Ollie, baby, we do know what it is that's been making you feel bad."

His gaze never left mine.

"You have an illness that is called cancer. There are different types of cancer, and the one you have is a brain tumor that you know about already, don't you?"

He nodded.

"Some brain tumors stop growing, and so when they take it out, it is gone for good. Some tumors grow back again. When they took yours out, sweetie, a teeny-weeny bit was left in because they couldn't get to it."

"A teeny-weeny bit?"

I nodded. "Yes, baby."

He held up a hand and made a small circle with thumb and finger. "Like this teeny-weeny?"

I laughed. "Well, kind of. Like I say, some tumors do grow back. Because we have this teeny-weeny piece left, it has been growing again. But they have really strong medicine called chemotherapy that is going to help you, and then you'll feel so much better."

Ollie repeated the word, "Chemotherapy," drawing out each syllable. "Okay, Mummy." He rubbed his eyes and yawned. "Can I go sleepies now? I'm tired."

"All right, sweetie. Lots of sleepies, okay? We have to be up early in the morning to go to the hospital for an MRI and see that nice Dr. Stew."

"Okay." With Ticky in hand, Ollie fell asleep.

Leaving the room, I sighed. It was done. I had introduced him to what lay ahead.

Now I had to tell Jess and George.

Together, Pete and I told Ollie's big sister and brother that Ollie had cancer, that he was going to have treatment involving radiation and chemotherapy, that he would lose his hair, and that the treatments themselves would make him sick yet ultimately better. We explained that it was going to take a long time and sometimes he'd have to stay overnight in the hospital. We told them Mummy would spend a lot of time away but friends in the neighborhood would help take care of them when Dad was at work. In order to protect them, we gave them only the need-to-know information.

They listened anxiously and asked questions, to which we responded honestly yet cautiously, not wanting to frighten them. We all shared hugs and said with determination, "Ollie's going to beat this thing. He's a fighter, and he will win."

"We are all in this together," I said. "Your dad and I, both of you, and Ollie. As a team, we are invincible." And I truly believed it.

∼⌒◯⌒∼

The next day we headed back to the hospital. Stew entered his room at Children's wearing one of his silly cartoon ties and a big smile.

Ollie stole a glance at the floor, presumably waiting for the Tootsie Rolls to fall out.

"Hey, guys. How are ya?" Stew shook Pete's hand and then patted me on the shoulder. "Hey, how ya doin' today?" He pulled up a swivel chair and rolled it over to Ollie. "We finally get to meet. My name's Stew." A gentle expression overtook his smile. "I'm gonna be taking care of you, buddy. I know you've not been feeling too good, but I'm gonna change that, okay?"

Shyly, Ollie sat and listened intently.

"Hey, so I hear you like trains. Thomas the Tank Engine is one you like, right? I have some of those at home and some other train videos. Would you like to see them?" He winked. "I'll bring 'em in for ya next time."

Ollie pretended to be disinterested and crossed his arms.

Stew looked at him with concern. "I know you're a smart kid. Your mum and dad told me, and I can tell. I know you've been feeling pretty bad, haven't you?"

Ollie nodded, tears appearing in his eyes.

"I know, buddy. I know. And I'm gonna help you. It's what I do, but you need to know that the medicine we give you is gonna make you feel pretty bad too." Calmly he explained what would be happening.

There was a look of realization on Ollie's face, as if he knew that what was inside of him was a *really bad thing*. Tears rolled down his cheeks, and he roughly wiped them away. He didn't yell or scream but turned his back to Stew, pulling at my heartstrings.

After our meeting with Stew, we made our way to the radiology department at Northwestern Memorial Hospital in downtown Chicago. Following a brief consultation with a Dr. Marymont, we were led to the area where Ollie would have his cast made and receive treatment.

The making of the cast was a lengthy procedure and required Ollie to remain perfectly still in a seated position as the radiologist wrapped a layer of cellophane around his head, neck, and torso, leaving small slits for his eyes, nose, and mouth.

When the wrapping got tight around Ollie's head, I sensed the panic in his demeanor and soothed him. I was grateful that the radiologist took breaks and even played with him, gaining Ollie's trust.

When the panic subsided, the radiologist painted over the cellophane with plaster of Paris. Several layers were required to ensure an effective cast. During radiation treatments, Ollie would lie facedown, the back half of the cast discarded, and radiation could be given to the specific areas needed.

The fact that Ollie had been inside an MRI unit helped when we were shown the radiation chamber, because this huge tunnel-like unit was similar. The stretcher bed with straps looked familiar except that it moved in all directions and was larger, like a long dinner table covered with sheets.

As Dr. Marymont explained the procedure of radiation therapy, I looked at Ollie and whispered, "This is a special table, Ollie. It's a magic table."

Fascinated, he looked at the table, then at me. "A magic table?"

I pressed my finger to my lips. "Yes. Shhhh. I will tell you more in a minute." I winked.

His eyes grew wider, his gaze fixed on the table.

When Dr. Marymont left the room, Ollie was eager to learn about the magic table. "Why is it magic, Mummy? What does it do?"

I remembered the times when each of my children had been scared about that first tooth coming out and I'd told them not to worry. "The tooth fairy will come, sprinkling magic dust and bearing a gift," I'd said.

Now I explained that only special children, ones like Ollie who hurt inside, got to lie on the magic table and it helped take away the hurt. "Because when you're on the magic table," I explained, "amazing beams of invisible lights will come down on your body. And they will not harm you, not at all, because the lights are good, magical, and healing."

Ollie stared at the table. "Whoa. And will you be with me, Mummy, when I go on the magic table?"

"I wish I could, sweetie, but I'm not allowed. Only special children like you get to lie on the table, but guess what? I will be right next door, in that room over there, and I'll be able to see you. This lady's going to show us how."

I wheeled Ollie's buggy out through the gigantic, heavy double door entrance to the chamber, and we turned a corner to find ourselves in a mini control area with flashing computer screens. Dr. Marymont flipped a switch, and hey presto, one of the monitors showed the magic table and whole chamber.

"See, Oliver?" Dr. Marymont said. "Mum can watch you from here! Shall we have Mum go back in so you can see her?"

He nodded, laughing. "Okaaay."

I went back into the chamber. Approaching the table, I pretended to be shocked to notice the camera. Unable to see Ollie's reaction, I felt silly, yet I didn't care. I knew he would be laughing at my antics. I pulled silly faces, posed like a model, then walked out of camera range, only to literally jump back in and mouth, "Ta-da!"

Suddenly we knew we could talk to each other via an intercom system, because Ollie's voice then came through loudly, "You're silly."

Amid his giggles, I pretended to jump out of my skin.

Captivated, Ollie couldn't wait to get started and try the magic table.

CHAPTER 5
Ella and the Cop with a Heart

After therapy began, we decided that having a pet might help Ollie and give the whole family a boost. No one was more excited than Ollie, who wanted a kitty. At the adoption center, he cooed like a bird at the cats and kittens that meowed for his attention.

One caught his eye: a young cat who lay cowering in the corner of her cage. Around five months old, she had a white belly and paws, with a mixture of tan and black covering the rest of her body. Despite her lovely coloring, her coat was dirty and lusterless, and her eyes were lifeless and dull. Silent, with not a single meow or a purr, she seemed miserable.

Ollie peered into the cage, his fingers poking through the holes. "C'mon, baby, c'mon. It's okay. Oh, you poor thing. C'mon. It's all right. I promise." His voice was soft, gentle, and coaxing. "Mummy, this kitty is scared. We have to take care of it. Can I hold it? What's its name, Mummy?"

The information tag revealed her name, Ella, and that she had been rescued from abusive owners.

I told Ollie, "It says here that Ella is not happy because her owners were not nice to her when she was a baby but that when she knows you, she's loving and will sit and cuddle up to you."

He continued looking at Ella, who now had lifted her head and was quietly watching him. He repeated, "I want to hold her, Mummy."

Attempts to fulfill his request proved fruitless as Ella sat frightened and hissing.

Ollie was undeterred, his heart obviously captured by her.

After a frantic struggle, we managed to secure Ella in the travel box and headed home, Ollie cooing at her all the way.

In the kitchen, I opened the box.

Ella leapt out, immediately making a beeline for the basement.

Oh, that's just bloody brilliant! I thought. *Now we'll never see her.*

For three days she hid there, and for three days, despite his extreme discomfort, Ollie would slowly edge his way down the stairs, one step at a time, bringing with him tidbits for Ella to eat. He left a trail of fish treats, starting just short of her whiskers, finishing up in front of his head as he lay on his tummy quietly coaxing her.

He would stay with her for most of the day, then slowly climb the stairs back to the kitchen, wincing in pain. Such was his pride and determination, though, that he would not let me carry him. Once at the table he'd flop into his chair, exhausted as he exclaimed, "Phew! That was tough work climbing those stairs. I need to rest now."

His understanding of Ella's trauma, her fear, and his need to help clearly demonstrated his patient kindness. Any thoughts for himself, his own struggles, he always put aside.

Even at bedtime he worried for her. "It's dark in the basement, Mummy. Will she be okay? Do you think we should put a night-light on?"

I stroked his adorable, concerned face, saying, "Baby, she'll be fine. It's nice and quiet for her, and besides, cats can see in the dark. I think she's going to be okay. I really do. You're taking such good care of her."

His face brightened. Comforted, he settled down for the night.

His persistent kindness would pay off. One morning Ella came out slowly, her nose twitching as she sniffed the air.

Ollie lay waiting.

Inching closer, she sniffed his hand.

Ollie stifled a squeal of delight, looked at me with bright eyes, and whispered, "She's licking my hand, Mummy. Look."

It was just the beginning of a special friendship. Ella would become a contented, sleek, and shiny pet with bright eyes and a personality to match.

Our normal routine before cancer treatments had been more or less the same as most people's: up at six, lay the table, eat breakfast, pack lunches, wash, brush teeth, prep bags, and head out the door to the school bus stop.

Now the routine was the same except that Ollie would vomit instead of eating breakfast. As we entered the fourth week of radiation, he stopped eating altogether. He'd always been tiny in frame anyway, and with his weight plummeting, he was skeletal in appearance.

I also needed to rise earlier to pack Jess's and George's lunches before I got Ollie out of bed. That way I could tend to him while the other two ate breakfast.

Pete was now working in New York, visiting only once or twice a month unless we had an emergency, so I was coping alone.

I'd give Ollie his various pain medications: Zofran for nausea, meds for constipation, and creams to help heal the burns. Then I'd prepare him for the drive downtown for treatments, and I'd drive him back home, which became nightmarish as Ollie's health spiraled downward. I was well prepared for our car journeys: vomit tray, urine bottle, wet wipes, towel, blanket, and pillow along with water. I would soon learn the fastest lane in which to switch and would become one of those terribly annoying drivers who'd cut in at a moment's notice, leaving a trail of irate drivers as I tried to get to the ER or home as fast as I could.

I recall one occasion when Ollie was extremely sick, and I knew the journey would only make things worse. On this day, we were barely moving when he became extremely distressed. He was so weak he could barely speak, yet I recognized the anxious murmurs along with his frightened gaze as he pointed at the vomit tray.

"Okay, baby, okay, I'm gonna stop, okay? It's all right, sweetie," I said. "Hang on, hang on."

Putting on my turn signal, I pulled over.

I climbed to the back and managed to get to him just in time.

The foul, yellow-green liquid, just one of the many side effects of therapy he endured, spewed into the tray.

When he was done, he looked at me with his wonderful brown eyes and said in his English accent, "Well, thank goodness that's over with. That's really horrible."

Laughing, I stroked his beautiful bald head and kissed it. "You're funny, little man. You really are, and I so love you."

"But, Mummy, I think I need to go poohs. Like

soon." His expression suddenly changed to one of worry.

We did not have a bedpan. We had tried that before, and it simply did not work, so we had agreed that whenever we were in the car he would wear a diaper—and it was to be our secret. Ollie did not want anyone to know, such was his dignity.

For some reason, though, this time I had forgotten to put a diaper on him. I silently cursed my stupidity. Cleaning up his vomit, I reassured him I'd get him home as fast as possible.

As I drove, cutting in at every opportunity, Ollie was getting more and more anxious. We still had miles to go, and I knew he wouldn't make it. I pulled over to the inside lane reserved for emergency vehicles and sped up, passing the virtually standstill lines of traffic.

Ollie thought this was hilarious and was waving happily to the passing motorists as we sped by. "Bye-bye. See you later." He giggled, the knowledge that we would be home soon obviously perking him up.

Looking in my rearview mirror, I saw flashing lights. I was in trouble. "Shit," I said out loud.

Ollie told me off. "Mummy, that's a bad word." He frowned.

"Sorry, baby, but there's a policeman behind us, and I have to stop."

I was panic-stricken. What if I lost my license? I rolled down my window as the officer approached.

"Good afternoon, ma'am. Do you mind telling

me why you're traveling in this lane? I clocked you doing ninety miles an hour." With notepad in hand, he frowned as he looked at me. "Can I see your driver's license, please?"

Nervously, I replied, "I'm really sorry, Officer. I'm just trying to get my son home. He's really sick. I'm sorry." Rather pathetically, I added, "I won't do it again."

"Well, I'm real sorry 'bout that, ma'am, but . . ." His voice trailed off as he took a peek in the back and saw Ollie, whose appearance was clearly shocking.

Extremely thin, weighing just thirty-seven pounds, bald, with burn marks from the radiation, his eyes sunken and grey, Ollie looked miserable.

The officer leaned toward my window again and, visibly moved, inquired, "What's your boy's name, ma'am?"

"Ollie. We're on our way back from Children's, and he's desperate for the bathroom, and I have nothing for him in the car."

The officer looked on compassionately. Putting away his notepad, he asked, "Where are you trying to get to? Traffic sure is bad today."

Perplexed, I answered, "Downers Grove. Why?"

He replied, "Well, ma'am, I'm gonna keep you and Ollie in my prayers. Let me help you get home." He smiled.

Observing his genuine concern for my son, I fought back tears.

With sirens blazing and lights flashing, this kind-hearted police officer escorted us home.

Ollie, who squealed with delight all the way, made it to the bathroom in the nick of time, dignity intact.

At the dinner table, I shared this moment with the kids while Ollie giggled.

Later on the phone, Ollie told Pete, who laughed and was just as touched as I was.

Random acts of kindness like these gave me a boost, yet as evening fell I would crawl into bed with one eye open and ears pricked for the slightest noise, any indication that Ollie needed me. My mind would replay the day, plan the next, worry for the kids, wallow in self-pity, and then get annoyed for having done so. I learned to sleep in spurts, sometimes staying awake all night for fear that I would doze through an emergency.

In turmoil, I would drift to sleep through the assurance of the baby intercom, which strangely I had kept since Ollie's infancy. I would hear in my dreams the sound of the pump that fed him overnight, his only source of nutrition, then be awakened by the strange gurgling sound of Ollie bleeding when his platelets were low and his blood wasn't congealing.

As I carried him from the bed, the blood would drip out of his nose onto his favorite teddy bears and stuffed animals, me, and the floor to the bathroom. Setting him on the toilet, I'd pinch his nose the way our home nurse had shown me. Invariably, the blood would run down the back of his throat. With terrified eyes, he would choke and spew huge clots, spraying my face. If I wasn't able to control the flow, then it would be another mad dash to the ER for a transfusion.

I became an expert on all aspects of treatments: their effect on complete blood counts (CBCs), signs of medical danger, responses required, and the fastest route to the emergency room. I once drove ninety miles an hour in the middle of the night as Ollie lay in the back bleeding out profusely, his counts dangerously low. Upon arrival, I rushed in carrying my child and people stared openmouthed, shocked at the bloody scene as I blurted out his desperate need for a transfusion.

Over time I developed a reputation with the residents and staff. During yet another mad dash into the ER, I loudly made my presence known.

When someone asked who I was, I overheard the seasoned ER nurse's reply. "That's Mrs. Tibbles. Tread lightly. She can be difficult at times, but you know what? She's a fantastic mother, and her son Ollie is just the cutest kid, level four medulloblastoma. They're in here a lot."

I felt grateful, indebted to them for understanding our plight and my often erratic behavior in protection of my child. Their kindness gave me strength on days I felt weak.

How I found the spirit to start each morning astounded me. Where was it coming from?

Life went on, and guilt set in. I was acutely aware that as time passed and Ollie's therapy continued, my focus was more on him and I felt I was neglecting Jess and George.

I sat with the two older kids to share my feelings that I was sorry we weren't able to spend much time together. "I hope you guys understand that it's not because I don't love you or want to hang out with you. You do know that, don't you?"

They nodded in unison.

"It's okay, Mum," Jess said. "We know you have to take care of Ollie right now."

George rested his head against my shoulder. "He's gonna be all right, isn't he, Mummy?"

I squeezed his hand. "Well, he is a sick little boy, and he does have a long way to go, but yeah, he's going to be fine, sweetie. You'll see. What's happening right now with him—all the sickness and stuff—is normal. It's what we expected. But he will get better. You know, if it were one of you guys, I'd be doing exactly the same thing. I love you all. You're all my babies."

They smiled.

"It might not be often, but I promise to find time where it's just us guys, okay?"

George climbed off the couch. "Oh. Can't it be

just you and me, Mummy? I don't want Jessica with us," he said jokingly.

"George, you're a pooh!" Jess jumped off the couch and gave chase.

George laughed and shouted, "And you're a smelly pants!"

I smiled, thankful to see some things hadn't changed.

❧

Quality time with Pete was also sparse, moments of intimacy few. In truth, our love life was the furthest thing from my mind. Of course, I had more important things to worry about, yet I wondered why I didn't want to seek solace in my husband's arms. In the early years, our relationship had been one of deep love and passion. Why was I changing? What was happening to us?

I pushed the questions away, making a sad realization: This was not the first time I'd had such thoughts. They had been coming and going for several years. Old familiar feelings had been stirring, with wants and needs I'd almost forgotten as I'd welcomed motherhood and the role of housewife and closed the door in my mind to anything else. Why were they resurfacing now?

So began our distancing. We were together yet slowly drifting apart. We were on the same journey, the same train, but in a different spot. As I saw it, I was up front, struggling in the control room with Ollie.

Pete was in a carriage farther back, supporting us and hoping he'd eventually join us. I prayed that somehow it would someday all make sense and we'd find a happy place as we rode this journey out.

One day, I noticed a change in Ollie: a spark. When I looked into his eyes, I did not see a dullness that one might expect from such a sick child. His beautiful brown eyes were bright, like a dark pool of water in the moonlight that you could dive into. There was something else about those eyes: a quiet knowledge, a secret awareness that didn't fit his young years.

Look into my eyes, Mummy, he seemed to say. *Can't you see?*

He was getting better.

Subtle changes were occurring that I wouldn't have noticed if I'd focused solely on the side effects of his treatment. He wasn't crawling to get around yet was tentatively and sporadically walking, no longer wincing at the pain. From the floor where he played with his train set, he would crawl to the side table and pull himself up, something he hadn't had the strength to do in months. He was also talking more, giggling.

Seeing him play with his brother again brought tears to my eyes. It had been so long.

In our dining room stood an old oak table. Upon it the boys had set up a train station along with tracks, trains, and a village full of people. On the floor, using videocassettes, they'd built a makeshift tunnel with strategically placed cars and trucks.

In our pre-cancer life, I'd had strict rules. The dining room had been out of bounds. I'd often commanded, "Don't play in there. You'll mark the table," or "Too loud, boys!"

Ollie would cheekily respond, "But, Mum, I'm four!"

I no longer cared about the noise. Now I welcomed it. I couldn't give a flying monkey about the table getting marked or plush carpet getting spoilt.

Happily, I watched the boys noisily playing while Ella sat under the table, hoping they'd throw her a toy.

Yes, Ollie's eyes said more to me than any words could. I dove right into those deep pools and received his message. I saw and knew.

Our journey so far had seemed like a one-way trip, hurtling out of control like a runaway train, its driver merciless, unyielding, laughing at our ineptness, slapping the wheel heartily, taunting, "Baby, don't fear the reaper. Come on, baby, take my hand . . ."

Now our journey was slower, calm. We had made a switch to a different track. I sensed it. The bold, fantastic awareness made my skin tingle.

As we neared the end of 2002 and of the first course of treatments, MRIs were scheduled and Pete flew in from New York to join me for the results.

In reception, we nervously waited for Stew.

Striding down the hallway, the clown with a big grin and a white coat approached and gave us a thumbs-up. Merrily waving the X-rays, he said, "Come on in, guys. I have good news."

Sitting down, he pointed at the screen and compared the images with those taken prior to treatment.

It was visibly evident. Ollie had responded to therapy. The tumors were shrinking!

It was nothing short of a miracle, and I wanted to throw my arms around this kind clown and cover him in kisses.

We knew it was not over and we still had one final stage of therapy to go through, but it didn't matter, for our son was getting better.

We left Children's in a euphoric state.

The sun shone brighter that day, and our smiles were contagious as people sensed our joy.

Our child was going to live.

CHAPTER 6
I'm Going to Be a Train

We were walking on air. Ollie was doing well and sharing the gift Stew had given us: he was being a kid again. It was September now, and he would happily join his brother on the school bus, play, and even ride his bike, which had been gathering dust in the garage since he'd received it on his birthday back in June. Everything was a blessing.

Happily, we shared our news with family and friends. We could feel their joy, see it on their faces. Our spirits soared.

It was a wonderful time, and a second gift would come our way: the gift of a wish.

We had been introduced to the Make-A-Wish Foundation when Ollie became a patient of Stew's.

It was explained to us that any child with a life-threatening illness is eligible for a wish. The foundation grants thousands each year, giving kids and families much hope and strength as they battle their conditions.

Brian Murphy, a wish granter for the foundation at that time, came to visit with Ollie on numerous occasions. His purpose was to find out as much as he could about him: his favorite color, games, foods, and sweets and what he would like more than anything in the world to do.

Brian could immediately see Ollie's love of trains. Sets were everywhere in our home, and often when he visited, Ollie would be watching a train video of some sort, usually *Thomas the Tank Engine* while choo-chooing loudly as he played. Ella would often accompany him, usually stretching across the tracks, to which Ollie would playfully scowl.

I could sense in Brian a kindness, a nurturing soul.

Ollie was very comfortable around him and would invite him to sit and play or watch one of his favorite train videos, of which he had many.

When we'd first arrived in the US, we could no longer watch our videos from the UK as they weren't compatible with the US video players, so we'd had to buy new ones. The first time Ollie pushed play on a *Thomas the Tank Engine* video we'd purchased, he was shocked when Thomas started to speak.

"That's not Thomas," he yelled indignantly.

I chuckled at his cute annoyance. He was right. Based on the stories British Reverend Wilbert Awdry wrote for his grandson, the Thomas the Tank Engine video series was originally narrated by Ringo Starr of The Beatles. A new American voice had replaced the soft tones of Ringo, and Ollie was most perturbed. Of course, by now he'd gotten used to the different accent.

Another set of videos he enjoyed starred the famous Dave Hood from the children's entertainment world. He produced a whole bunch: *There Goes a Fire Truck, There Goes an Airplane, There Goes a Police Car*, and many more. It was during one of the times at Children's that Ollie discovered them. In the videos, Dave portrays himself rather idiotically, goofing around and creating mayhem as he not only entertains but also educates kids. Ollie would watch them over and over, laughing at Dave Hood's silly antics.

Even Brian and I couldn't help but laugh at the silly yet clever story lines Dave Hood and his crew came up with.

When Brian explained the idea of a wish, Ollie

didn't truly comprehend what it meant. At first he asked if he could have a new toy train or maybe a set of railroad tracks or maybe a caboose. It took some time to register and a few meetings with the calm and accommodating Brian.

Ollie's big, brown eyes grew wide in amazement when he finally understood.

Brian chuckled at his sudden realization and shot me a wink.

Ollie said in disbelief, "So I can do anything I want, Mummy? Go somewhere, like a holiday or something? Visit Grandma and Granddad in England even?" He bounced on his seat. "Go to Disney World?"

I nodded. "Anything you want, sweetie."

"Is there anything you can think of, Ollie? Anything at all that you would like to do most in the whole world? Even if you think it's not possible. 'Cause you're a kid, I know. But even if it's something you think only a grown-up can do, just say it, okay? Remember, the Make-A-Wish people have special powers. They can make anything happen. They make dreams come true."

With a smile, Brian chimed in, "Your mum's right, Ollie. We can make anything happen for you."

He thought about this for a bit and asked again, "Anything?"

"Anything."

What he finally said did not surprise me. "I want to be a train driver."

Brian grinned, and I hugged Ollie.

"Of course you do." Looking into Ollie's eyes, I recalled a question I had asked him when he was about four years old, a question all parents ask their children: "What do you want to be when you grow up?"

"I'm going to be a train."

I laughed. "You mean you want to be a train driver, right?"

He put his hands on his hips, looking at me as though I were bonkers. "No. I want to be a train, silly, and I'm going to be someday."

As he shook his head, I scooped him up in my arms and twirled him around. "You're such a funny little man, and I love you!"

He promptly kissed me on the lips with a *muah* noise. "And I love you, Mummy, always and forever." He rubbed his nose against mine, something we always did after a kiss.

Now here we were planning his wish, and Ollie wanted to be a train driver. It made perfect sense. When asked the train he wanted to drive, he said, "The super-duper cool Metra passenger train. The one that's a double-decker, like the red buses we have in England. Can I, Mummy? Can I?" He said it as if he didn't quite believe he actually could.

"Of course. The Make-A-Wish Foundation can make anything happen. They have magical powers!"

Brian was ecstatic. "Well, I'm not surprised by this at all, Ollie. It's perfect for you, and what a wonderful privilege that I get to be involved." He was positively gleeful and enthusiastically began making the plans to grant the wish he fondly referred to as "a typical young boy's dream," one he himself would've made as a child.

And lengthy plans they were. Permission had to be granted from both Metra and BNSF (Burlington Northern Santa Fe) Railway Company. Representatives from both companies were touched by Ollie's wish and pulled out all the stops to ensure all arrangements ran smoothly. Metra even had an engineer's uniform made in Ollie's size.

When news of his wish spread through the train community, retired ticket conductors and engineers asked to be involved and wanted to meet this brave child who shared their love of trains.

We decided the best time for the big day would be that spring, when Ollie's therapy concluded.

Brian set a date, April 5, 2003, now six months down the road. I just hoped Ollie could wait that long, such was his excitement.

Stew allowed us a much-needed break from therapy, and I was grateful. I wanted Ollie to have a rest, to get stronger for the next round, to be normal for a while.

With Halloween approaching, we eagerly got into the spirit. Aside from Christmas, Halloween was Ollie's favorite holiday. We bought three pumpkins, and Pete helped the kids carve fun faces into them.

More festive decorating ensued. Cobwebs, spiders, ghouls, and spooky lanterns delighted the kids from around the neighborhood who came to admire the creepy scene. Ollie's face lit up as he looked at the scene from his buggy, where he sat wrapped in his special quilt.

The blanket was a beautiful gift from our friends in the neighborhood. They had all gotten together and made it while we'd been at Great Ormond Street in London. Decorated in Ollie's favorite theme, Thomas the Tank Engine with its reds and blues, each patch was a gift from an individual family we knew. The words *I love you* aplenty, a prayer, a child's handprint—all were carefully hand sewn with care. Ollie adored that blanket and took it everywhere, wrapping himself in the love of it.

Sitting in the driveway outside the garage on Halloween night, he was cocooned in his quilt while we set up lounge chairs next to him. A table was set up holding a stereo and of course a huge witch's cauldron full of goodies for the kids trick-or-treating.

When kids passed by, Ollie would hit the scary music button on the stereo and laugh when they jumped.

That year, George was Spider-Man, Jess was Dracula, and Pete was a boring fart. No costume for him, much to the disappointment of the kids. I was a rather too convincing witch doctor with my real-life syringes, white coat, rubber gloves, and scary makeup. I had the toddlers clinging to their mummies. Ollie loved it.

Ollie dressed as Harry Potter. At the school Halloween parade, Ollie's aides had proudly pushed him around in his buggy to a cheering crowd of family and friends. He'd smiled the entire time.

Till now, we had been too busy "to-ing and fro-ing" from Children's to fully discuss his diagnosis with the personnel at his school. I set up a meeting to do this in person with all staff present.

Of course, their reaction was entirely what I expected. They absorbed the information with complete support for us. They wanted to help Ollie and serve him the best way possible so that he could remain the happy child he was.

Since his body was still frail, I explained what was normal and what the danger signs were, what a port is and how it's used, and that he didn't like it to be touched. I demonstrated how to lift him up without coming into contact with it. I stressed the importance of an aide accompanying him outside for recess and asked them to call me immediately if he bled but to call an ambulance if he stopped breathing.

I was eager for him to be treated like any normal kid, and they assured me he would be. Their care and dedication to Ollie helped him enormously. Knowing he loved to ride the school bus, they secured him and George a place up front for easy access. Even if he could only attend for a few hours, he loved school.

In this wonderful place of learning, he became somewhat of a celebrity, his black buggy and Thomas rucksack a familiar sight as he made his way down the hallway with Mrs. S., his favorite aide, toward the library or computer room.

Children would smile, wave, and call, "Hey, Ollie, how ya doin'?"

He would wave back or give his cheeky monkey grin.

When either collecting Ollie or dropping him off at school, I would always be touched to see so many children of all ages coming up to give him a high five as they passed heading into a class.

Kids from different grades, some of whom he didn't actually know, witnessed his struggles and his courage. Without realizing it, teachers and students alike found themselves learning lifelong lessons from an unexpected source.

❧

While the staff and most students were supportive, as we all know, children can sometimes be cruel. One day I got a call from Maryanne Sanfilipp, the principal at Willow Creek.

"Mrs. Tibbles? I'm afraid there was an altercation on the bus this morning. Unfortunately, I've had to suspend George from riding the bus for one day. I know it's an inconvenience, with him taking care of Ollie, but I have to follow school policy when something like this happens."

George? Altercation? I was bewildered. This was not like George. "What happened? Is he okay? Is Ollie okay?"

She explained that a new boy, who was a year younger than George, had been making fun of Ollie on the bus, calling him names and poking both him and George despite their repeated requests to stop. Other kids on the bus verified this. Upon leaving the bus, the boy continued his taunts. George swung round, hitting the boy in the face with his SpongeBob SquarePants plastic lunch box.

I was shocked. None of my kids had expressed themselves this way ever. It was certainly out of character for George, but I understood why he'd done it.

I thanked the principal for informing me and told her I would talk to George about it when he got home.

When the familiar yellow bus pulled to a stop at our corner, I watched George carefully help Ollie off the bus, holding his rucksack and his hand as Ollie gingerly came down the steps one at a time.

I found myself watery eyed. George was always taking care of his little brother.

As he entered the kitchen, I could tell he was wondering what I would say and if I might give him a telling off.

How could I? He had simply stood up to the bully to protect his brother.

I surprised him with a hug, telling him how proud I was that he'd stood up for Ollie. Hitting someone was really not the way to do it, I added, but I loved him and was proud of him anyway.

We all thought he was a hero and none more so than Ollie.

With the occasional transfusion or infection here and there, our life resumed. What many of us might consider mundane each day, I embraced as quite the opposite. I had a newfound appreciation for things I had barely noticed before, things I had taken for granted: birdsong, the rustle of trees, the perfection of my son's toes, the blue sky, a stranger's smile, the crackle of a fire at night, the feel of a cup of hot cocoa warming my hands, and my children's breathing as they lay sleeping. It was as though my senses had been reawakened. With the blinders taken off, suddenly I could see, and it was glorious. Mundane reigned supreme.

CHAPTER 7
Train Days

It was Christmas 2002, and Ollie was reveling in feeling nearly normal. His happiness was contagious, energizing all of us. With my newfound vigor, I not only set out the over-the-top Christmas decorations but was motivated to return to work.

My passion for group fitness had begun after Jess's birth, and over the years I'd become certified in various fitness disciplines. I had given up work to care for Ollie, and my boss had said if I ever felt like coming in I should give her a call. Periodically we kept in touch. The outpouring of love and support from my work colleagues and members was tremendous, and I found I missed them greatly.

As we made arrangements for my return to teaching, I was suddenly nervous. Not just because it had been so long, but I wondered if my stamina would survive. *Shit*, I thought. *Too many bloody cigarettes.* And how would I react to questions I knew would be asked about Ollie? I desperately hoped I could control my emotions and not end up a blubbering mess.

I walked into the studio shaking and was greeted by cheers. My emotions swelled, tears threatening.

Thankfully, one of the members yelled, "C'mon, Deb! Let's get this show on the road. We need a kick-arse class! We've missed you."

With hugs and smiles, I donned the mic, hit the music, and let the magic happen.

It was an amazing experience. The members gave more to me in that class than I gave to them. It meant so much to be able to teach a class, get out of the house, and be wrapped in their support. To forget, for a couple of hours, the traumas of the preceding months was a terrific boost to me spiritually as well as physically.

It was also good for Ollie and the kids. I had always taught, and my return represented routine and security, just as Ollie's return to school had done.

Some days as I embraced the mundane, I could almost imagine cancer wasn't happening.

The routine frequently gave us a false sense of security. Out of nowhere, it would be replaced by havoc.

As we entered the next phase of treatment, yet another

unyielding infection tore into our son. His courage astounded me. His selfless kindness was humbling.

When he sensed my fears, he would invite me to sit with him and a wise soul would emerge. "It's going to be okay, Mummy," he would say as he lay on my lap, gently stroking my hand with Ticky. "It's going to be okay," he'd repeat in barely a whisper, and then he'd smile.

He seemed to know something I did not. A secret. The kind that makes you feel warm and special. Important. And it was as if his knowing was enough; he didn't need to share.

His quiet words comforted me. I never questioned but simply embraced them and was strengthened.

Ollie marveled at the simplicity of life too: his own breath on a winter's day, how the sun made him squint, the reflection of his shadow, the sounds of nature. He giggled at the bunnies romping in our yard as they played chase.

We would sit together on the swing that hung from our tree in the back garden. We'd hum along in unison to the rhythm of its swaying, our song interrupted only by the occasional command, "Higher, Mummy. Higher!"

As the final phase of therapy drew near, I focused on the MRI images we had seen earlier: the shrinking tumors, evil retreating from my brave fighting child. I took solace in Ollie's words that everything would be okay.

On days when fear tried to taunt me as my son's body grew ravaged once more, he battled on. He would smile weakly and ask to ride the train.

Off we'd go, complete with a pack of supplies for any unexpected hiccups. For Ollie, bringing the pack became as normal as carrying a bag of his favorite chips.

Riding the train was Ollie's favorite pastime, and we were a common sight on the ride to Chicago and back again. Ollie chatted with the ticket guys, who came to know him and let him wear their conductor hats as they told him about different types of trains. Ollie was both envious and impressed by one conductor who told him he had a caboose in his backyard and invited him to come see it one day. Ollie looked on in wonder as though Santa had arrived to play when another conductor showed him photographs of his train village in his basement.

Passengers had a mixed reaction to the sight of Ollie. Some would turn their heads as we approached. Others stared in shock or pity, but most smiled kindly as Ollie smiled back.

Children asked questions like, "Why don't you have any hair?"

Ollie would respond, "Because I have cancer."

"What's cancer?"

"It's a sickness. I'm sick."

The children would shrug and say, "Oh, okay. So what's your name?"

Happily they would chat, innocence prevailing.

This happened several times, and more than once a mother would appear embarrassed and quietly apologize for her child.

"Oh, please, so not necessary," I'd respond, smiling.

Some days Ollie only wanted to sit on the platform, wrapped in his quilt in his buggy, watching the trains as they passed. He waved at the passengers, who waved back.

I noticed how trains were almost magical. Businesspeople in suits or travelers in sweatshirts would smile and wave at the stranger waving at them. In that one moment, they were not worrying about their day, their lives, their struggles. In that instant, they were engaging with another human being, connecting with no agenda, just *being* with each other. They didn't question the moment, yet it magically lifted them— and it lifted us.

When Ollie asked for train days, I felt there was a purpose, though I didn't quite know what it was. Like an itch you can't quite reach, I could not figure it out. I was just aware that it was there, present.

I remembered when we'd taken him to visit Thomas the Tank Engine and Friends in Union, Illinois, on a rare family day trip out. Like all the other kids, he was excited to meet his train heroes. We roamed the train museum with him in his buggy, wandering through each coach from eras past. He was back to his childlike fascination, carefully taking in all of the train information we read to him while his sister videoed the day's events.

His train days now were different. *He* was different. Despite the chill in the air, we would sit in warm silence, time of no consequence as he held my hand.

In the tranquility of those special moments, I felt incredibly alive, my emotions swirling. I felt enlightened but penitent. Joyfully I drank in simple pleasures as Ollie did, yet I also felt guilty that I had failed to notice them before. I was ashamed of how I'd behaved in the past: yelling at my kids for no real reason, taking for granted the lifestyle my husband worked so hard for us to enjoy, allowing my ego to develop at work and forgetting what teaching was truly all about. I felt remorse at the ignorance I had sometimes displayed when someone had reached out to me and I hadn't wanted to get involved. I lamented that I'd sometimes preferred the company of my girlfriends to a family night at the movies or day out together. I regretted that I had not faced up to the truth of our marriage—of myself—but had let Pete and everyone think we were a-okay. I was disappointed to realize that when it came down to it, I was terrified of going it alone, of losing the big home and those white picket fences that contained so much promise yet left me feeling trapped.

In those moments on the platform, I saw myself with an ugly clarity and wanted to retreat home to my comfortable world and shun the unwelcome intrusion into my soul.

I could not leave, though, for it was always Ollie who decided the right time to leave. I wondered if he could see what I was seeing, feel what I was feeling. Did he know my deepest thoughts?

As our journey continued through the final rocky terrain of therapy, the New Year was upon us and excitement was building as Ollie's wish drew near. Although the CBCs revealed Ollie's increasing fragility, you would not know it by his demeanor.

Breathlessly, he would tell all and sundry about his special day. "I'm going to be a train driver, you know. I have a uniform and everything. *And* I will be famous because I'll be the youngest train driver that ever lived. You can read about it in the papers if you want," he'd say with his cheeky monkey grin.

We'd all laugh, but he was right. Somehow the local media had gotten wind of the story. The press, both television and radio, would be present along with the mayor of Downers Grove. While the rest of us were super impressed with the news, Ollie didn't bat an eyelid but just smiled.

I knew his wish was spurring him on, giving him strength, lifting him.

I prayed we wouldn't move off course. "Please, God, if you are listening, please let him have his wish. Allow his dream to come true, I beg of you."

Someone else was tuning in to my prayer, lurking. Evil smirked and fiendishly switched tracks. Rubbing its hands and sneering, it marveled at its wickedness. Oh, it was *so good*, for we barely noticed. We were unaware we were being sent in a horrifying direction that would have us fighting for control as we hurtled into a place we had never been: one we had not considered.

We were blissfully ignorant, caught up in those images of shrinking cancer, in our son's joy, in the love and support of family and community, in the hope instilled by a clown in a white coat.

And evil winked.

CHAPTER 8
Jess and George

I was worried. Both Jess and George had missed homework assignments, their grades were dropping, and they hadn't been themselves lately.

Jessica had been having frequent mood swings and choosing to stay locked in her room. One could say this was normal teenage behavior, yet Jess had typically liked to hang with us. Even though she had her own TV, she'd always enjoyed watching movies in our family room.

She'd also been staying overnight with friends. At first, I'd welcomed the sleepovers. They gave me less to worry about, and I knew she was going to have a good time. Then I learned they were for a different reason.

One day, while she was at school, I found her journal on her dresser. I felt reading it was not about checking up on her but about protecting and understanding her. I had seen it before but had never felt an urgency to peek inside. This time was different. The drive was strong, so I opened and began reading.

I HATE CANCER was written in bold, dark letters.

Short sentences were left hanging. Words jumped out at me:

Why is this happening?

SCARED.

SAD.

Can't talk to Mum.

I saw short passages of anger about when a family outing got put on the shelf as Ollie was admitted with yet another infection.

It's so UNFAIR.

He's so brave.

Mum and Dad don't hold hands anymore.

I HATE CANCER.

The words screamed off the page.

Tears welled in my eyes.

The truth behind Jessica's distance was written here. She didn't always like to be around Ollie. She found it hard to witness his struggles, and she became irritated when I needed her to help me and she couldn't escape to someone's house.

She could see it all, and I hadn't noticed. I had failed as a parent. I felt guilty. Not for intruding on her innermost thoughts. No, I felt ashamed because I hadn't been there for her. Being so consumed in the care of her brother, I had neglected her, my precious child, my sweet, beautiful Jessica. My mind drifted to her introduction to our lives.

We lived in a small apartment in Greenwich, London. We were broke yet happy because Pete had just landed a new job. Things were on the up and up.

We spent a night celebrating with friends. With wine flowing through our veins, we later frolicked in the bed and, though I was on the pill, Jessica secretly settled into my womb.

I can recall waking two days later with a strange feeling. My body was still experiencing some aftereffects of our night of debauchery days earlier. I just knew it was something other than pregnancy. Putting the kettle on, I tucked the thought away with a shrug and a note to myself, *Don't mix wine with liquor*, then got busy making breakfast. Opening the fridge, I saw we were out of eggs. "Bloody hell."

I yelled at Pete, who was still in bed, that I'd be back with eggs and I left for the store.

Returning home, I headed to the bathroom. Unwrapping the box I'd bought, I took out the spatula-like implement and sat on the loo. Turning on the tap to help urge my urine, which was not forthcoming, I waited, looking between my legs, trying to keep the spatula still in my shaky hand. Eventually, the pee came and the grey plus sign turned a pretty pink.

I wandered into the bedroom, where a bleary-eyed Pete tried to make sense of the spatula I was waving in front of him.

Grinning like a Cheshire cat, I said proudly, "I'm pregnant."

"Oh, shit," came his reply. His initial shock soon gave way to joy.

Despite the turmoil that would later hit us personally and financially, we embraced parenthood and basked in the sunshine of family love as our parents awaited the arrival of their first grandchild.

I had a nauseating pregnancy, yet I relished it. I was instantly enamored the moment I felt the baby stir inside me and later, following an exhausting labor, held Jess on my chest. My journey into motherhood had begun.

The unplanned arrival of Jessica changed me

in so many ways—as a friend, as a daughter, as a sister, as a mother, as a human being. Her birth changed my destiny.

I reflected on our years with Jessica, the ease of her being when she'd slept through the night at three months. No matter the constant ear infections to which she seemed privy, she would never complain. She would play with Boppa, her plastic bouncy friend that when blown up was as big as her one-year frame. We would set it down next to her, looking rather like an oversized Weeble that would bounce right back up each time it was pushed down, amid Jess's gales of laughter.

Later, she would paint her toenails like Mummy or wear my heels. We loved our days in the park, riding the donkeys on Sundays, feeding the squirrels. I remembered her first day at school and how she'd run excitedly while I'd tried to hold it together.

To her, moving to America had been a fantastic adventure and she'd happily settled into her new life, making friends easily with her social butterfly temperament.

With blurry eyes, I closed the diary and felt as though someone had captured the butterfly in a jar.

With tired and wounded wings, she flitted pitifully, and I desperately wished I could release her. Helplessness once again enveloped me.

I was so tired. Tired of it all. It was never ending: the bloody trauma, the not knowing. One minute was transparently inspiring, the next darkly void.

Then there were the add-ons that came unexpectedly, like the do-gooders from the local church who shared that praying to Jesus was the answer via a cake left on the doorstep with a Psalm. I'd thrown the cake away, thrown the support away, not wanting to recognize the hidden message: *Your child is going to die, and I am preparing you, thinking of you, and we are here.*

I opened the diary.

I HATE CANCER.

I was one with my daughter.

Closing it, I sighed.

I would not look into her diary again.

I had failed to realize how much my children saw and heard. They knew. I had not given them enough credit for their insight. I could have learned much from them. They were pure, innocent, untarnished by the world as adults viewed it.

Worse, somewhere along the way I'd lost sight

of the child who lived in me—that silent presence that begged my ear, my heart, and wanted to come out to play. Like every other adult, I'd sent that child to the corner with a bright shiny dunce cap. Now Jess, at such a young age, was learning to do the same. Suddenly the low grades and attitude didn't matter. What mattered was making sure Jess never put on that damn cap.

I vowed to talk to her. Clearly, I would not reveal that I had read her diary, but I wanted to make amends to her and also to George, because suddenly I remembered that he too was behaving out of character.

The incident on the school bus had been a sign of George's frustrations. Like his sister, he was missing homework assignments and having outbursts of cockiness that were so unlike him.

George's way of handling things was different. He wanted to spend as much time as he could with his brother. On days when Ollie wasn't well enough to attend school, George would ask to stay home with him. If that didn't work, he'd feign sickness.

George had barely known life without Ollie. Just two years apart, they were inseparable. Prior to Ollie's diagnosis, they were always getting into mischief together, the way all boys do.

George was around three when they began sharing a room. Often after the bedtime story and lights-out, I'd hear them trying to play quietly. I would creep up the stairs for the tenth time to tell them, "Go to sleep," and smile at the sound of little feet running as they jumped back into bed. Opening the door, I would find them with their eyes closed tight as they tried not to move an inch. Invariably, one of them would give in and giggles would ensue.

George, I could sense, was missing those times. Ollie's health was now so fragile, his energy sparse, and George just wanted to be there on the good days.

I thought about our first days with George.

George arrived three years after Jessica, loudly screaming as he came into the world. As a baby, he could not have been more different from our calm, easygoing Jess. He cried constantly, had severe colic, and was not sleeping through the night until his toddler years. Sometimes the only way we could get him to sleep was for his dad to strap him in the baby seat and drive around aimlessly, whatever the hour. Sometimes we would give him warm baths and rock him to sleep.

We continued to be sleep deprived because George had night frights. They were terrifying to his dad and me. He would go into a trancelike state, with a look of horror on his face, screaming in fear, often sleepwalking and eventually vomiting. We took him to the doctor countless times, afraid he had some horrible illness. When I look back, it couldn't have been more ironic. Yet we learned that this was normal behavior for a child suffering walking nightmares.

In a way it made sense. George has a vivid imagination that was reflected in the pictures he drew, so intricate in their interpretation, and the movies to which he was drawn. One such movie was *The Nightmare Before Christmas*, which he would watch over and over and to this day remains one of his favorites.

When he was born, Jessica was so excited about having a baby brother. She loved to help me take care of him, even when he was screaming. In those early years, they shared a room and, unbelievably, Jess got used to the pandemonium that would erupt when his frights came at night. She slept peacefully all the way through. George's night terrors would eventually leave him, and my first special boy—and we—would finally get an uninterrupted night's sleep.

He shone at school, though getting him there in the first place was traumatic. Unlike his sister, who bounced her way into the classroom like Tigger, George clung to me like a leech and pleaded to stay home, suddenly complaining his tummy hurt.

"Mummy. Mummy. My tummy. It hurts, Mummy. It hurts."

And his teacher would have to pry him off me, slowly and carefully, like a Band-Aid that's been there too long.

"Don't leave me, Mummy. Don't leave me."

As I waved, I'd yell a cheery, "I love you, Georgie. Have a lovely day. See you soon." And I would make a hasty exit so he couldn't see my pained face.

How different these two wonderful children, like chalk and cheese, yet they were entwined in their anguish for their brother.

I would allow George his time with Ollie whenever he wanted. I called the school principal to put her in the picture, hoping she would be okay with it.

Thankfully, she was. Compassionate, she understood the importance. Her tone was soft, not the usual disciplined voice to which I had grown accustomed. It was as though she knew the time was short and school would still be there *after*.

Knowing how desperately Jess and George needed it, Pete and I made every effort to have quality time with them. We called upon our army of supporters, our friends in the neighborhood, to watch over the kids so we could spend time with each individually. Pete was not traveling as much for work now, so some days he would stay home and I would take special alone time with each child.

With Ollie's condition in control of our lives, time together was often unpredictable. We were on a mystery train ride into the unknown, one minute blazing with sunshine and laughter, the next dark and scary as we hung on for dear life. We rode it out the best we could.

CHAPTER 9
Wish Day

In early March, with Ollie's wish now just weeks away, we took Ollie to Stew for the medical clearance to proceed with the special day. Oblivious to the examination taking place, Ollie excitedly described how he was going to drive the big passenger train.

Stew feigned shock. "Well, I just don't believe it! I don't think a kid has ever driven a train before. You'll be famous."

"I know!" Ollie smiled.

Stew signed the papers clearing Ollie for the wish despite the final round of therapy he had yet to undergo.

Ollie would complete the treatment bravely.

Though his body was acutely fragile, he was undeterred. With great enthusiasm, he talked nonstop of only one thing to his nurses, family, and friends. His dream was coming true. He was going to be a train driver.

It's amazing how the power of a wish affects a sick child. There is no doubt in my mind that this wonderful fantasy for which he yearned lifted him to a higher level, affording him the joy and strength he'd need as he spiraled toward something terrible of which none of us were aware.

Three days after Ollie's therapy ended, we were back on the 4 West Ward at Children's. Ollie had a high fever and cramps. CBCs revealed he was neutropenic (zero white count), meaning he was at great risk of overwhelming infection and required hospital treatment with antibiotics. Ollie also urgently needed blood and platelets. Both were transfused, and strong antibiotics were administered to combat his infection. He also had C. diff again.

Pete and I settled into our usual rotation of shifts, one at home, one at the hospital. Ollie would stay for three weeks. Finally, when his counts started to rise and reached an acceptable level, we were released to continue his medical care at home under the supervision of Stew and our home nurse, Maureen.

We knew it could take weeks and several more transfusions before the counts would climb. We had a chalkboard in our room where we would mark the numbers each day. In the past, Maureen had come once a week to change Ollie's dressings and check his vitals, yet now she was coming almost every other day. As always, she came armed with an abundance of stickers and candy, which Ollie accepted with a weak smile.

Four days after Ollie was released, his fever spiked and we were back at Children's for yet more blood and platelets. I wondered how a child could possibly need so much. I knew children typically could heal and produce new cells with speed, whereas adults healed slowly. It unnerved me. This was the first time Ollie had needed transfusions so quickly, and along with them came another unyielding infection.

I was heavy with his suffering, standing helplessly on the sidelines, feeling desperately alone. In my mind's eye, I felt as though I were standing in the middle of the railroad tracks and his train was leaving without me, disappearing slowly into the distance. As so often happens in weird dreams, I was rooted to the spot, legs buried in cement, unable to move. Frantically I yelled a voiceless cry, *Don't leave me, Ollie!* The train silently moved on and became barely visible while evil rubbed its hands.

I wondered how much more Ollie could take. The ensuing infections were wreaking havoc, and it was clear to all of us that his tolerance for the toxic chemicals was lessening.

Still Ollie smiled.

Though my instinct told me he would eventually leave us, I still had a glimmer of hope that maybe he would be that miracle child who stunned the medical world. If anyone could, I truly believed it would be Ollie.

Alongside hope stood mother instinct, my comrades in love and pain. I knew them well. If instinct proved to be right, then I wanted to have as much time as possible with Ollie before he left this world. Hope fueled my soul on days I felt depleted.

Pete and I discussed our fears about our brave child who had battled so hard and gone through so much this past year. Would he be well enough to experience the dream he so richly deserved and desperately needed?

Please, God, please, we each silently begged.

Tentatively I broached the subject Pete had always pushed aside, refusing to discuss—Ollie's life. How long did he have? Would he even survive to drive the train?

It was a cruel, ghastly dilemma that was almost unspeakable. Never in our most terrifying of nightmares had we imagined a discussion of this nature: the death of our child. The horror was knowing—living with death and making plans for it as we would for an upcoming birthday party. But unlike a planned celebration, this date that loomed invisible would not include balloons or kids running around and eating too much cake while the parents complained that their children had consumed too much sugar and would be awake half the night. Oh, for the joy of such parties and petty worries!

I took breaks between the questions I never wanted to ask Pete. I thought if I gave him some time to *think,* he would respond, yet he remained silent, shaking his head, his shoulders weighed down.

Our comrade hope stepped in, not wanting either of us to make those wretched plans, and I was grateful.

After a time, Pete spoke. "He's not done yet, Deb, and we still have options. They're bringing out all sorts of therapies, new drugs, all the time. You know what Stew said about the research. They're coming up with new ideas, and you never know, Deb. One of those could be the one. The one that really does kill it. He could be the miracle kid who shows them all."

With hope by his side, Pete vowed to do anything and everything he could. He wanted to exhaust all the options Stew offered in order to save his son.

Though my heart ached from the tug-of-war between hope and mother instinct, Pete's resolve gave me the strength to push the dark thoughts away.

~◌◦◌~

Brian Murphy from Make-A-Wish kept in touch regularly, updating me on the wish day itself and what would be happening.

Speaking with Brian, I expressed my concerns about Ollie's failing health and my concerns that he might not be well enough for the wish to go ahead. He understood, stressing that if Ollie was too sick on the day, it didn't matter. The foundation would simply reschedule.

It was a relief to know this option was available. I wanted Ollie to know it too, so I explained it to him.

He was adamant. "I want to do it now, Mummy, even if I'm sick, okay? I'll be fine. I just know I will."

I nodded and smiled. "Okay, baby."

Ollie was two months shy of his seventh birthday.

During the course of therapy, throughout the innumerable stays in the hospital, he had grown wise far beyond his age. His sense, his perception of things, seemed to be growing, and I was in awe of him. He was enduring and unafraid, and he wanted me to know it.

"I love you, Mummy, always and forever," he would say with a huge, relaxed sigh as he rested his head on my lap. Stroking my hand with Ticky, he would constantly tell me he loved me and everything would be all right and I need not worry.

In those moments I felt as though an old soul was speaking. The words came with a kindness and clarity that did not seem to fit this young child who just over a year before had been running around in the playground. His quiet awareness made me uneasy. He seemed so adult, and I yearned for the young boy in him to return. Where had my child gone? Where were his cheeky monkey grin and playful innocence?

The day prior to Ollie's wish, a flicker of that innocence returned. The excitement of the day was the only topic of conversation. Thankfully, in those moments, his reflective thoughts were forgotten.

The course of high-dose medication he was on

to fight his infection was almost complete, and the horrible effects had been decreasing. Even in his fragile state, he would be able to enjoy his wish. The mere idea of it spurred him on. Of that I had no doubt.

The lengthy preparations were now complete. Liaising with Brian from Make-A-Wish and representatives from Metra and BNSF, we were set to go.

Days before the wish, Brian had stopped by with the special engineer uniform and hat Metra and BNSF had made. Ollie couldn't wait to put them on. He loved them, and they gave him a wonderful boost.

All of our family and friends would don the T-shirts I had made with the Make-A-Wish logo. The shirts showed a cute, smiling boy sitting on his red tricycle, with the bell that went tring-tring-tring-tring. Underneath were the words *Oliver's Wish. April 5, 2003. Where dreams come true.*

I made sure when ordering that we had enough for Ollie's classmates because I felt sure the whole school would turn out. On April 4, I went to collect the T-shirts from the local shop and took out my credit card to pay.

The owner waved a hand at me, saying, "That's not necessary. My prayers are with you and your family, Debi. I hope Ollie has a great day." He added with a smile, "I hope to be at the station when he comes in."

Fighting tears, I thanked him and marveled at the beauty of the human spirit.

When I got home, I took out one of the T-shirts and held it up. As I stared at the date, something occurred to me that I hadn't even realized when we'd set the wish date with Brian.

April 5, 2003 was wish day. Ollie's mother tumor had been removed exactly one year earlier, on April 5, 2002. I smiled, feeling that in some strange way this was appropriate and right on time.

⁓⌇⁓

Wish day began with the arrival of a limousine to transport us to Chicago Union Station, where Ollie was greeted by Metra and BNSF officials as well as the train engineer who would accompany him and ticket collectors and retired conductors who wanted to be a part of this child's dream. All were people who loved trains as much as Ollie did.

In his buggy Ollie sat, decked out in his miniature uniform and proudly holding his stopwatch presented to him by the train engineer.

"After all, trains need to be on time, don't they, Ollie?"

Ollie giggled before responding, "Of course!"

He happily posed for pictures with the engineer, conductors, BNSF officials, and Make-A-Wish volunteers before boarding. That day the train had an extra carriage right up front reserved especially for family, friends, and volunteers. Make-A-Wish had decorated that same carriage inside and out with balloons, streamers, and train pictures so that as the train whizzed past people would know something special was happening.

It would not be a private trip but one of the regularly scheduled commuter services that would stop at each station, giving those who boarded an opportunity to share in the power of a boy's wish. Unwittingly, these passengers would be granted a gift of spirit, a shot of inspiration in their otherwise normal routine. Following Ollie's wish, we would receive messages from strangers who found themselves touched by Ollie, his courage, and the tremendous outpouring of love so evident that day.

Pete carried Ollie as we boarded.

A surprise awaited. Dave Hood, his hero from *There Goes a Train,* was along for the ride. Ollie practically gawked in disbelief and wonder. He turned to me and said, "It's him, Mummy! It's him!" It was fantastic.

Pete and I knew a few days prior to wish day that Dave would be attending. The foundation had contacted him, and he'd said he'd be honored to come along. He'd flown in from San Diego especially for the occasion.

When Dave saw Ollie for the first time, I thought I saw him wince at Ollie's frailty, yet he smiled broadly as he greeted him with an abundance of goodies. He sat next to Ollie for most of the journey, and they chatted like old friends, pointing toward the window. Every now and then Ollie would giggle, clearly at some joke Dave had made. When Dave presented him with his entire There Goes a . . . video series, Ollie's mouth fell open.

With family and friends enjoying the ride, the train clickety-clacked out of the city toward our hometown of Downers Grove.

It was all so marvelous. A wonderful sense of happiness seemed to float in the air throughout the journey. At each stop, people cheered and waved, and Ollie weakly waved back, his smile strong and permanent.

Ollie's school principal, his teachers, and his aides were along for the journey, taking turns to come and spend time with him and snap photographs as keepsakes of the special day. Ollie joked about how famous he would be and that they'd better keep those pictures for the newspapers, and we all laughed.

Finally, the moment of Ollie's wish was upon him. The engineer approached him, telling him he was needed in the engine room. He explained to Ollie that it was against normal procedure for us to enter the engine room, but the rule was being graciously set aside for his wish.

This was true. We'd learned from Metra that for safety reasons, only engineers and train staff were allowed in the engine room. Written permission had been granted by BNSF headquarters to allow this unprecedented event to take place.

When Ollie, Pete, Jess, George, Mr. Hood, and I entered the engine room, it was so incredibly loud that it almost hurt our ears. I momentarily panicked, thinking the noise would upset Ollie. However, he had lost a lot of hearing due to the effects of therapy and wasn't bothered in the slightest. We all donned massive earphones to block out the thunderous noise.

Ollie sat on his dad's lap, admiring the lighted control panel before him.

Seeing Ollie's gaze drawn to a large, red button, the engineer smiled and nodded. "Go ahead!"

Ollie looked at that button for an age, as if savoring the moment. It looked like the kind of anticipation you'd have at the mere thought of something so irresistible to your palate you'd drool. He continued to gaze, then looked up at the huge window and the tracks that lay before him. Finally, he pressed that big red button.

Oh, how that glorious train horn blew!

He pressed again and again as we cheered him on. Applause could be heard faintly from the carriage behind us as family and friends realized Ollie was at the helm.

In that one precious instant, his suffering and pain were gone. In that moment of innocent dreams, my boy was just that: a boy living his dream.

We all felt it. A warm veil of happiness, peace, and love embraced all of us in that engine room. I knew, without a shadow of a doubt, Ollie was in that moment the happiest I had ever seen him. I struggled to fight back tears of joy.

❦

As we approached the Downers Grove station, we returned to our seats.

Though the day was beginning to catch up with him, Ollie remained in high spirits.

We anticipated a large crowd of familiar faces. Our friends in the neighborhood were gathering with banners. Many kids from Willow Creek School, along with their families, would be wearing their T-shirts and waiting eagerly to cheer as the train pulled in. The mayor of Downers Grove would also greet us, and there would be a huge party inside the station with gifts, cards, and a train-shaped cake.

We knew all of this, yet we were completely and utterly unprepared for the sheer volume of people waiting.

As the giant Metra train gracefully pulled to a stop, the speaker blared for all to hear, "From Chicago Union Station, the Oliver Tibbles Express has arrived!" The illuminated passenger information box above the crowd displayed the same message.

Familiar faces seemed lost in this sea of people, this ocean of support and love for a child most had never met, all sharing this child's wish. The poignancy of a boy's simple dream to be a train driver was enough. Some, with tissues in hand, dabbed their teary eyes.

I carried Ollie, whose head rested on my shoulder, through the train's open silver doors.

The crowd chanted, "Well done, Ollie. We love you, Oliver! You go, Ollie," as we disembarked to the sound of popping cameras and the flash of lights. Cameramen and journalists jostled for a good spot.

I turned to make sure my family would not be lost in the throng and briefly glanced at Brian from Make-A-Wish, who raised his eyebrows and shot me a grin. I hoped he understood my smile in return as I silently thanked him.

The train pulled out, honking its horn, and we walked into the station. The mayor of Downers Grove and hundreds who'd waited patiently greeted us with cheers.

We sat at an allocated table where people lined up to meet Ollie to give words of love and share in the magic of the day. Some, many of whom were strangers, arrived bearing gifts. It was incredibly touching to observe this kindness, this genuine care for a small boy, and I found it difficult to stay composed. There was a beautiful aura around us all, one I believe we'd all failed to notice in our fast-paced lives: the human spirit. That day, it was thriving.

After a while, I knew Ollie was exhausted by the day's events. As I held him in my arms, he nestled his head against my neck and whispered, "I want to go home now, Mummy."

Pete, Jess, and George could see how tired Ollie was and understood it was best that he and I leave and have some quiet time before they got home. They'd stay to meet and greet all who had come, sharing their own experiences of the day with friends and strangers alike along with various members of the media.

The crowd cheered and waved their banners as Chicagoland's most famous engineer bade them a happy farewell.

Ollie lay peacefully on the couch, his infusion safely administered.

I covered him with his special quilt, tucked Ticky under his arm, and kissed his forehead.

Sleepily, he gazed up at me and said, "I'm famous."

"I know you are, baby."

"I want to rest now. I'm tired. Soooo tired, Mummy."

"Okay, sweetie, you have a nice long sleepies, okay? I love you, baby."

Almost immediately he was sound asleep. I hoped he was dreaming of trains with miles of track ahead as he sped gloriously along to a place of child fantasy, of warmth and sunshine, where suffering and pain did not reside, where only peace and happiness grew in abundance as he frolicked in sweet joy riding his own magical track.

The following week saw Ollie recover well from his infection, and he spent happy hours playing with his brother with the gifts showered on him the day of his wish, including eight new train sets.

All around the lower floor of our home, he and George set them up. You could not walk through the house without tripping over a tunnel or stepping on a train, a piece of track, or a conductor with a raised flag. They even placed stations on the kitchen counter and would move from room to room, their imaginations running wild. Even Ella had to carefully sidestep the newly constructed towns and stations with a slightly put-out meow when the boys chastised her playfully. It was bloody marvelous.

Amidst the joy, evil would interrupt, taunting me with its presence. I focused on the good, trying desperately to pull hope back, yet that familiar looming presence was getting stronger and more powerful, leering at my weakness, shoving the question into my mind savagely without mercy: *When will he die?*

No one answered. I saw it as a good thing that I received no response, as if hope was still around, a cherished friend visiting and not wanting to leave.

Life continued. The yellow bus came and went. People emerged out of hibernation from the long winter as spring arrived.

We busily made plans for Georgie's ninth

birthday party at Chuck E. Cheese's coming up May 1. He chose the invitations and excitedly handed them out at school.

Of course we hoped Ollie would be well enough to attend, but if it turned out he wasn't, the party would still go on and I would stay home with Ollie. I would feel bad for George if this turned out to be the case, yet at the same time I didn't want him to miss out. My first special boy understood completely.

One day while Jess and George were at school, I was doing laundry, folding clothes from the dryer. Ollie was in the family room watching *Blue's Clues*. Every now and then I heard him join the game they were playing. "There! There's a clue!"

Moments later I heard a noise behind me and turned to see Ollie crawling naked toward his bathroom, the one I had allocated to him to help keep germs at a minimum.

I'd never realized until my son got sick the power of germs and how easily they spread. Frighteningly, for Ollie a simple handshake could equate to a life-threatening infection. Sometimes kids visiting would forget to wash their hands, yet my protective maternal instinct would always kick in. I'd pounce like a cat and scoop them up and into the bathroom to scrub. I'd even add a little

Lysol spray to their clothing. Parents would laugh, and the kids were actually okay with my eccentric British behavior. Like all innocent kids, they just knew. Eventually, so that the kids could avoid being sprayed by the crazy mum, I had posted a sign: Ollie's Bathroom—Do Not Use.

As Ollie slowly crawled, he resembled a skeleton inching his way to the door. With a pang, I noticed his beautiful penis hanging limply, swinging to and fro as he edged closer, his double pic line dangling from his arm.

Observing my magnificent child with protruding bones and burnt skin, I felt something punch my heart with incredible force. It was as if I was made to watch in slow motion a movie of everything this precious child of mine would never have or experience. The thrill of a motorcycle or fast car as he pulled into our driveway, music blaring as I would yell, "For God's sake, Oliver, how can you hear yourself think with all that bloody racket?" Attending parties and calling to let us know he was okay and on his way home. He would be a thoughtful young adult, caring for those around him. That's how kids with cancer who survive turn out, and he would be one of those unique individuals. Butterflies of first love. Sexual awakening. The pleasure of such love. Holding a girl he adored on a warm summer evening. The love of his life whom he would marry. The child within him who awaited the doting father he would become. I envisioned him giving me a hug, this big hand-some fellow who, just like his dad, would not be embarrassed to give his mum a kiss.

I saw everything and knew in that instant that he would have none of it. Brutally the truth of his life lost ripped deep into my soul, and the pain of that sudden awareness sent me stumbling to the floor. Suddenly, I was barely breathing for the racks of sobs that viciously attacked me. I tried desperately to stifle my screams, knowing he was yards from me.

Somehow I managed to call my friend just four doors down. "I . . . need . . . you . . . to . . . come."

Toni arrived minutes later and played with Ollie while I sat on the toilet upstairs, burying my head in my hands, succumbing to what I had known all along yet had not been ready to accept.

Ollie was going to die.

After a time—I don't know how long—I wiped away snot and looked in the mirror. I didn't recognize myself. Someone else was sitting there. It felt strange, like I was out of my body looking at me, a different me, an empty, shell-like me. Inexplicably, flashes of my childhood came to mind, fast and furious, all at once.

Happy memories of the summer of 1976, the year of the heat wave in England. I remembered swimming in the warm, bath-like ocean with my mum, sister, and two brothers and our three dogs. Oh, how we played! Chasing each other along the water's edge, our feet sinking in the soft, wet sand.

I remembered my mum wearing this white towel turban typical of the seventies to protect her hair from the rays. I'd thought she looked both glamorous and idiotic at the same time. "You wouldn't see me dead in one of those," I joked with my sister Kaz.

I was the oldest, and Mum let me stay up Saturday nights to watch the weekly horror movie with her. She'd make me a cheese and Branston Pickle sandwich. When it was over I'd leap a mile to the bed, scared that a ghoulish hand would grab my ankle. Then I would sing in bed with my sister.

Mum would come in and declare, "Okay, girls, I think Saturday Night Palladium has closed for the evening."

We'd giggle.

I was often mean to my little sister, though, making her get up to turn the light off even though the switch was right above my head. Years later we would laugh hysterically at the memory of how she eventually got fed up and sat on my head, farted, and said quite firmly, "Turn it off yourself, you big meanie!"

Sitting there alone in the bathroom, I recalled the sad day our father left. I was five at the time. A few years later, Mum remarried a man who turned out to be an alcoholic. To protect us, Mum would lock us in our rooms so that only she would feel his wrath. If only microwaves had been invented back then, perhaps dinners wouldn't have been spoilt as my mum took a beating and I hid under the blankets, my pillow covering my ears.

I thought of the vile torment that would eventually come my way at the hands of a so-called friend, which would abruptly end my innocent childhood and taunt me long into my adulthood. An evening when my mother had gone out to celebrate her birthday and a male friend offered to babysit when our regular sitter could not. He liked to drink whiskey. To this day, I cannot stand the smell and the memories it stirs in me or even say his name.

He wore a cardigan, a sweater with a zip in the front. Being the eldest, I was allowed to stay up a bit late when my siblings had already gone to bed. A movie was playing: *The King and I* with Yul

Brynner. I used to love that movie. Now I cannot watch it.

I knew I was in trouble, sensing the way children do that something was not quite right, not *normal* when he said, "Come sit on my lap, Deborah," patting his knee. I told him I didn't want to, and he firmly responded, "Be a good girl and do as you're told."

I was ten years old and scared of what my mother would say if I didn't behave the way I was told, so I did as he asked. When I did, he wrapped that cardigan around me and zipped me in. I couldn't breathe and tried to wriggle out of it, which seemed to make things worse. He laughed and pulled me in closer.

I stopped wriggling then.

Much of what took place was a blur, my mind blocking the savagery of it as I wished over and over for it to end.

Physically, I would heal, yet mentally the scars would remain.

I thought of it all.

I thought of the sadness I felt at never truly knowing my father, never being Daddy's little girl. The disappointment when he would devastate the second most important woman in my life, Cari, my second mum, when he left her too.

I had loved Cari from the first moment I met her when I was seven years old. She was the only woman my dad had met who genuinely took an interest in all of his children. While his other girl-friends thought us all a nuisance during custody visits, Cari enjoyed spending time with us. Sometimes we would have a day out with our dad, just us four and him, yet mostly it would be a weekend or the odd week here and there with Dad and Cari, and we loved it. All of us bonded with her and affectionately came to know her as our second mum. Some forty-odd years later, we still think of her that way, despite their parting.

Then I remembered the utter bewilderment and loss when I called to tell Dad of Ollie's diagnosis and he replied, "It's taken *this* to get you to call me?" I'd hung up and shut him out of my life again.

Grabbing a piece of tissue, I blew my nose and sighed. Still looking at myself, I reflected on my past, my fortysomething years. I thought of Ollie, the one precious thing in my life that was honest and pure. I thought about his short life to date and tried not to burst. Staring at the person before me, I wondered, *Am I not worthy of this child? Is that why he suffers? Is that why he'll be taken away from me? What did I do wrong?*

My childhood may not have been a fairy tale,

yet it was mine and I owned it. It was part of my destiny, and I believed paths crossed for a reason, connections were made that impacted my life, even when I didn't understand them or when they seemed cruel. If I had not traveled the road of my youth in the way it was given, I would not have found myself where I was today. I could have steered in an altogether different direction, not met the people I had, not fallen in love with the man I'd chosen, not given birth to my three beautiful children.

I would not have had my Ollie.

Spent from wallowing in self-pity at the loss I knew would eventually come, I splashed my face with water and with absolute hatred thought of the uninvited guest that had entered my child's brain.

Evil would want me to feel that way, I realized.

A surge of love for my child pushed the hatred aside. I challenged evil.

Yeah, you sure chose the wrong mother to fuck with, you bastard. You really did. And guess what, you son of a bitch. You can't have him, and my son will die happy.

CHAPTER 10
Train Wreck

Days later Jess and George were home from school
and busily doing their homework while I prepared
dinner. Draining the water from the cooked po-
tatoes over the sink, I looked out into our garden. The kids from the neighborhood rode their
bikes around the cul-de-sac while parents mowed
their lawns. The scent of fresh cut grass came in
from the open window. Squirrels chased each other
across our deck, eagerly feasting on the nuts Ollie
had put out for them. Ella was perched on her stool
in the screen room, just off the kitchen, watching
intently with her ears pricked and meowing when
the squirrels came near.

Life was busy being busy.

As the radio hummed a mellow tune, from the family room came a terrifying yell: "Mum! Mum, Ollie's bleeding!"

I rushed in and saw George, his face ashen, staring in horror at the sight before him.

"Oh my God!" I went to Ollie, whose shirt was soaked and red, his nose bleeding profusely.

Jess frantically tried to clean up the blood with tissues but looked helpless as they had no effect whatsoever. Tearfully, she cried, "He's bleeding, Mum, and I can't get it to stop. What do I do?"

Ollie's eyes were wide with terror, and he was trying to speak. "Mummy! Urrghh, nooo. Help me!"

His look, frightened and bewildered, reached inside me. This child trusted his mother above anyone else, believed she always had the answers. With Mummy, everything would be all right.

His look asked, *What's happening to me, Mummy?* and I had no answers.

George was rooted to the spot, a statue with tears.

"George, go grab me a towel from upstairs, one of the big ones, okay? Quickly, George, quickly!" I ordered.

As if woken from a trance, George dashed upstairs.

Blood was everywhere. Ollie was swallowing it and then vomiting it back up, thick black globs spewing from his red mouth and teeth, spraying Jess, the furniture, and me. Dark chunks landed on the cream carpet, and crazily I wondered how I'd get the stain out.

As Jess tried to ease the flow, I called Toni for the second time. "Toni, I need you here. I gotta get Ollie to the ER. He won't stop bleeding. Come quick," I yelled.

Surely sensing the terror in my voice, she arrived minutes later.

I knew Children's was the best place yet feared he wouldn't make it.

Toni called some friends to watch over Jess and George, then drove us as fast as she could to The Good Samaritan, our local hospital. I sat in the back with Ollie, who continued to bleed.

It took fifteen minutes. He had been bleeding for almost thirty. Ollie was no longer speaking, and the blood continued to flow as if his life was leaving him, fading right before my eyes. I kept talking to him, trying to keep him with us, and the only response I got was a tiny flutter of his eyelids and horrible gurgling from his lips. Soon they stopped fluttering, and a deathly silence took over.

My nightmare had arrived. He was crashing.

On arrival, the doctors' looks of both shock and pity at Ollie's appearance spoke volumes.

Quickly, the staff got a drip going, made him comfortable, checked his vitals, and took labs.

Toni, a seasoned nurse herself, whispered, "He needs to be at Children's."

Her statement frightened me. Good Sam's was not a pediatric facility. After all of the previous times spent in an ER, I was acutely aware that something truly terrible was in our midst and I wished I had gotten an ambulance direct to Children's. Why hadn't I done that? He was in the wrong place.

When the blood flow was finally at an end, Ollie lay in the ER, lifeless, connected to numerous tubes and monitors.

Finally, with the chaos and horror past, I had time to call Pete, who immediately left work to join us.

Toni stayed with me as we nervously waited for news.

When Pete arrived, we received a call in our room. It was Stew. "Guys, I'm having Ollie transported to Children's, okay? I know they're hydrating him and have some meds going, but he needs to be on the unit. I'm gonna order some blood and platelets too. We'll get him sorted out, okay?"

He did not go into detail about Ollie's condition that I suspected was fast becoming critical, and we didn't ask.

Numbly, we awaited transportation.

Ollie was still not conscious, but a moan would escape his lips here and there. He was still attached to the various lines and monitors, and the paramedics came in to collect him.

"He always did want to ride in an ambulance with lights on and everything," I said to the drivers, "yet the nurse said you wouldn't be doing that?"

One of the guys gave me a kind look and a wink. "Hey, I guess she must have been mistaken. You bet we'll have 'em on for your boy."

With lights flashing and sirens blaring, Ollie got another wish.

***

We arrived at Children's and were immediately taken into ICU isolation. Ollie's blood pressure was dropping, and he was still out, not responding when I said his name.

Nurses gathered in chaotic organization, changing lines, hooking him up to more powerful drugs, checking monitors. They spoke in unison, and I couldn't make sense of it.

Trying not to panic, I attempted to breathe slowly.

Pete left for the bathroom.

Suddenly and without warning, Ollie began

to shake violently, almost jumping on the bed as strange noises came out of his mouth, a horrible crunching noise as his teeth came together along with a sound I had never heard before, a primal wailing. I couldn't believe what I was witnessing or hearing, a wide-awake nightmare, my child the star of the show.

One of the nurses yelled, "Get Stew—now! He's seizing."

More nurses rushed in to try to get control of the situation.

I hovered in the corner. Helpless, I observed with tears in my eyes a scene I could never have imagined: my beautiful broken son shook uncontrollably on the bed, foam now coming out of his mouth, his eyeballs wildly rolling under his eyelids. His small, frail body took the full impact of the tonic-clonic seizure that gripped him for several minutes that seemed so much longer.

I noticed Ticky still clutched in his hand and felt myself burst as the sobs came out fast and furious. As the horrendous seizure continued and the sheets turned yellow-brown as his body succumbed, I found myself whispering, "Let this be over. Please, please, let him be all right. Oh, Jesus. Oh, God. When will it end? Don't go, Ollie. Baby, come on. Don't go, baby. Not now, not here. Come on, baby. Come on!"

The violence of the mother seizure stopped. However, he was still having mini seizures, and his blood pressure was now dropping at a frightening rate: 65/35, 45/15, 35/10.

Pete came back to the room, a look of horror on his face at the sight before him.

Our son did not look like our boy. This emaciated, skeleton-like child lay on the bed moaning intermittently.

Stew appeared, wearing a deadly serious look I had not seen before.

More doctors followed, filling the crowded room.

Immediately Stew put his arms around me while he looked at Ollie and the monitors and listened to the nurses relaying the details of the previous seizures and his current critical status.

Ollie's blood pressure was so low his body was unable to circulate blood, and his brain was starved of oxygen. His heart rate skyrocketed to almost two hundred beats per minute as it fought desperately for life. His respiration bounced back and forth erratically from forty to sixty, then plunged and rose again. This was it. Our nightmare had burst forth. Our precious, brave boy was descending into a dark nothingness, consumed by septic shock.

Stew looked at us. "He's not doing good. I'll come and talk to you in a bit, okay? We're gonna do all we can," he said, ushering us out of the unit.

The ICU is comprised of cubicles with curtains that separate each bed. At the far end of the unit is the critical room, where Ollie lay now: a glass-paneled room with several monitors, a constantly occupied mini nurses' station, medical supplies, and contraptions too numerous to mention. Some were unnervingly alien to me.

We watched through the window as our child lay spread-eagled on the bed surrounded by doctors and nurses battling to save him. We got only a brief glimpse of him before a nurse drew the curtains.

It was April 28, 2003.

In anguish, we paced.

After what seemed an eternity, Stew opened the door. "Hey, guys. Well, we've got him on epinephrine and dopamine to keep his blood pressure going. It's still critically low, but we've managed to stabilize him."

I searched his kind face, waiting for the reassurance that Ollie would be fine.

A pause. "I'll be honest with you. I'm real concerned. It's not good. This is what I feared." The sentence hung in the air as Pete and I clung to Stew's every word. "The next forty-eight hours are critical. If he can pull through . . ." He smiled faintly. "We know he's a fighter, our Ollie. If any-one can, it'll be him."

The three of us shared a moment of quietness, one of those necessary silences.

Then Stew told us what we didn't want to hear. "Guys, you have to know that he may not make it. I wish I could say otherwise, but the truth of the matter is I don't know. What I do know, as I've said to you before, is that some kids make it through septic shock and some don't. You need to try and prepare yourselves for that, make arrange-ments, just in case."

The finality of those kindly spoken words hit us like a freight train, and I wondered how long we'd be trapped in the wreckage and whether Ollie would make it out.

"When can we see him?" I asked tearfully.

"You can come and see him now."

We scrubbed our hands and donned gowns and masks.

Ollie still lay spread-eagle on the bed, naked. You could not see his genitals because his groin was swathed in bandages where enor-mous tubes had been inserted in each upper thigh to pump the lifesaving drugs. Another tube exited from his penis where a catheter had been placed, attached to a large bag for his urine that rested at the side of the bed.

His double lumen pic line from his arm was attached to a plastic contraption that fed extra lines, an adaptor of sorts, giving him vital fluids, saline, blood, and platelets. More lines had been inserted in his hands to feed powerful antibiotics to ward off potential infection, which if contracted now, would kill him. He was also on round-the-clock total pediatric nutrition. A tube had been inserted in his nose to pump oxygen. All across his chest and back were sticky pads, small sensors in place that connected him to the various monitors, mini television screens that constantly played the show of our son's life: poor ratings right now, yet we sat glued, praying they would get higher.

A nurse sat at the computer screen in the corner reading data. She smiled at us, and I was grateful she didn't speak.

Pete and I pulled up chairs and sat on opposite sides of the bed staring at our child, dabbing at our tears. We did not talk, each of us lost in thought.

With alarm, I realized Ollie didn't have Ticky with him. Now more than ever, I felt he needed it. Amidst all the chaos with the transportation team securing our bags, Ticky had been left behind. I looked at Pete and said, "I'm going to 4 West to get his things."

Pete nodded. He understood.

I hated to leave Ollie. The thought entered my head, *What if he dies? Like right now, just as I leave or while I'm in the elevator?* I dismissed it as quickly as it arose, and I can't explain it. My instinct told me it would be okay, nothing would happen. It was a feeling, a sense, something I just knew.

Leaving ICU, I headed to 4 West and the room we'd been allocated.

As I passed several of the nurses, I was aware of looks of pity. Some smiled softly and gently patted my shoulder.

"I'm so sorry to hear about Ollie."

"Good luck."

"Hang in there."

I nodded and smiled back. I had nothing to say.

I took out the can of Lysol and sprayed generously all around Ollie's rucksack and individually sprayed the items inside. Ticky was smeared with blood and other bodily fluids. I took it to the sink outside his room and washed it with the antibacterial soap that leaves your hands parched and red. I rinsed Ticky and hung it over one of the IV poles to dry.

"That's better. Ticky's all nice and clean now, Ollie," I said as I entered his unit. "Won't take long to dry, and then you can have him back, okay?"

I did not expect my son to respond, yet I knew he could hear me like a baby in a mother's womb who does not understand the words coming through like an echo but knows the lullaby, senses its love and sincerity, feels comforted, safe. Whether my son could hear the words I spoke didn't matter. I knew the echo of his mother's tone would be enough.

At the bedside, Pete and I stroked our son's hands and spoke to him. Pete talked about the lovely times they'd had together in the playroom on 4 West and how he was looking forward to the next craft project they would make together. I talked about what we would do together when summer came, of the pool and how he would learn to swim and cannonball off the diving board into the deep end. I reminded him that his birthday was coming up in June and of the fun party he would have at Chuck E. Cheese's with his brother, sister, and friends.

We put on his favorite videos, *Thomas the Tank Engine*, *There Goes a Train*, and *SpongeBob SquarePants*, and found ourselves laughing.

I told Ollie that Ella was missing him and was keeping his bed warm. We talked about everything, and silently we prayed. We talked and waited. Time passed. Hours into days, and I was grateful when they came. Hope was with us.

Sometimes I would go outside and smoke, watch the world go by in moments utterly surreal. I floated in and out of some crazy nightmare as life outside our hellish world continued.

My angry random thoughts targeted people innocently going about their days. *How can you smile when my child is dying? How can you laugh? How can you not know what's going on in here? Are you blind?*

Then I would sob out my rage, ashamed for begrudging them their happy, normal lives with their happy, living children. With a horrible clarity, I realized that if I allowed these feelings to fester, they would consume my soul and evil would win, and that was not up for negotiation.

Frequently Stew came into Ollie's room to check his condition, and every few hours or so a team of doctors and nurses paraded in, discussing the critical patient and his ongoing care. They sensitively would ask us if we had any questions, and we would smile and shake our heads.

We told our families and friends what was happening, yet we shared only part of the information with Jess and George. I didn't want to worry them any more than was necessary. I wanted to wait until we knew for sure. Our friends looking after them understood this and promised to keep it to themselves until we returned home, with or without Ollie.

Still he teetered; still we waited.

When news spread of Ollie's critical condition, some neighbors offered to come in and pray by his bedside. I refused. This may have been of comfort to someone else, but for me and his dad the idea had the complete opposite effect. To us it was like erecting a huge neon sign over his bed that read: I Am Dying. Sign Me Up, God. I wasn't ready for him to be signed up and was pissed off at God. I couldn't see the purpose of my child's suffering and ultimate death, which I feared was now imminent.

As far as I was concerned, God didn't give a shit. I wanted to punch God in the face. I kept these ugly thoughts to myself when I politely refused, not wanting to hurt well-meaning people's feelings. I knew their offer arose out of despair and care for us. The truth was, I was torn inside, one minute hurling foul rage at God, the next on my knees begging for mercy as I apologized for my wrath.

We kept our bedside vigil of speaking of Ollie's fun times ahead: seeing Ella again and Crabby, his new pet; going fishing with his dad;

riding the Metra train, the one he got to drive on his wish day. We told him how much we loved him, how proud we were of our brave soldier. As *Thomas the Tank Engine* played in the background, I reminded him of the passengers on the trains who missed that little boy who waved and how the conductors wanted him back on board.

For five days Ollie sat next to death, and on the sixth day hope surged unexpectedly.

While I held Ollie's hand, he squeezed mine. The tiny movement was the most powerful I had ever felt. My heart leapt as I looked at the monitors, which showed a small peak. His vitals were improving.

Pete had gone to grab a coffee, and I raced out to find him, yelling excitedly at the nurses and anyone passing as I went, "He squeezed my hand! Ollie squeezed my hand!"

Smiles and cheers erupted from nurses and patients' family members.

Pete dropped the coffee in the sink as he ran back to the room, entering with the biggest smile and hugging me.

We sat on either side of the bed looking at Ollie, then at the monitors. We saw another flicker of movement as his eyelids fluttered.

A small moan escaped his lips.

"Oh my God. Ollie? Ollie baby?" I soothed.

Suddenly the room was swamped with doctors and nurses, followed by Stew, who was grinning from ear to ear. While Stew and the team babbled excitedly, we focused only on Ollie as he opened his eyes.

"Mummeeeee?"

Tears rolled down my cheeks, and quickly I brushed them away as I responded, "Yes, baby, here I am. Daddy's here too." I squeezed his hand and kissed his forehead. Smiling, I gave a silent thank-you to God.

Ollie was back.

CHAPTER 11

The Summer of Love

Ollie was out of the darkness. He had survived what most don't, stunning the medical team. Doctors, nurses, and interns paraded into his room, feverishly taking down notes, openly staring at this deathly sick child with a shake of their heads as he sat in bed watching *SpongeBob SquarePants* and giggling.

While the team discussed this medical miracle, I gave hope thanks and the Universe a wink.

Ollie had returned to life for us the day before George's birthday in 2003, and I often wonder at that. Was it coincidental, or was this yet another sign? Everything in my being was saying yes, it was a sign, and it made sense. Selflessly, kindly, Ollie wanted to be there for his brother's birthday.

When I called to share the good news with our kids, George returned that kindness when he said, "Mummy? I don't want to have my birthday party, not without Ollie, and I don't want to open my presents until he comes home."

My heart went out to him. "Oh, sweetie, are you sure? You really don't want a party?"

"I just don't feel like it, Mummy." Then he said, "Can I bring my presents to the hospital and open them with Ollie? And bring the cake?"

Tears stung my eyes. "Let me talk to Stew and ask him. We might have to get special permission, but I have a feeling it will be fine."

I could picture him nodding and smiling. "Okay, good."

Pete and I took turns talking to Jess and George about Ollie: what they could expect to see when they visited, that it would be several weeks before he could return home, and that we were hoping to transfer to 4 West soon. Mostly, we focused on telling them how much Ollie had missed them and couldn't wait to see them.

After Stew gave the all clear, George celebrated his birthday in the hospital. Ollie's eyes lit up at seeing his brother and sister, and George gave Ollie his presents to open. We sang happy birthday to George and watched videos.

I listened to the banter of our three children with a heart bursting with joy. *Thank you, God. Thank you.*

When we met with Stew, we asked many questions, the first being, "When can we go home?"

"Recovering from toxic shock takes time," he said. "We need to see improved readings for his BP as well as his other vitals. Even then, he needs to be weaned off epinephrine and dopamine gradually until eventually he's able to circulate the blood by himself."

Pete and I nodded, listening intently.

"I'm going to put him on medication to combat the seizures because the likelihood of him having more is high, though you probably won't even notice them. As you know, the major seizure he had has affected his motor skills and some of his senses. Over time, they will improve. Further down the road, we can look at physical therapy and hearing aids for the hearing loss."

We had noticed that the hearing loss had increased, yet amazingly it did not seem to bother Ollie in the slightest. Quite the contrary, in fact.

When someone tried to be heard in his presence, they would begin to shout as we so often do when talking to someone hard of hearing while making those ridiculous faces, stretching our mouths wide, talking in slow motion. Ollie found this quite hilarious and desperately attempted to hide his amusement by covering his mouth. Invariably he would fail and giggles would win, leaving the person perplexed and embarrassed. Those were great moments.

Stew continued. "He's going to need constant blood and platelet transfusions until we see a rise in counts. Right now his white count is still at zero, so I've got him on Neupogen. A few more weeks and, provided he doesn't pick up an infection, you guys are out of here." He smiled.

"What happens now?" Pete said.

I wished he hadn't asked. *Don't go there, Pete. Not now. Not yet.* I wanted to enjoy this time of healing, of Ollie coming *back*, of winning the battle, of survival. I didn't want him to fight anymore, didn't want him to be my brave soldier. *Put down your weapons, my son. It's time to come home.* I just wanted him to be a normal kid again.

Stew seemed to read my mind. "Well, right now, let's just focus on getting him home. He could do with a break, I think, and regain some strength to be a kid for a while. Later we can talk more about our options going forward." His gentle smile was reassuring.

Pete didn't press the issue.

Two weeks later, we moved out of ICU back into 4 West. Ollie smiled and waved like royalty amid the nurses' rousing cheers.

Each day, Ollie got stronger. Each sunrise brought a new blessing: a rise in counts, fewer transfusions, coming off the nutrition infusion, no infections, his wanting to eat food for the first time in almost a year. After all he'd endured, culminating in his knocking at death's door, it felt as though he had been reborn. His downy new hair confirmed it.

Finally in early June, we waved a cheery goodbye to 4 West and left for home.

The summer of all summers, the summer of love, began with the arrival of our family from England. Our home was filled with the chaotic joy and mayhem of six children—ages three, seven, eight, nine, twelve, and fourteen—and eight adults.

Ollie was tumor free, line free, and bouncy happy. Each day was a new adventure.

Out of the blue, however, we succumbed to a

horrible sickness that my family brought from the UK. One by one, we fell like flies—all except Ollie.

I was the last to hit the deck, and I hit it hard, confined to bed with a high fever, sweats, and puking my guts up for almost a week. For a year I'd cared for my son on little or no sleep and never once gotten sick. It seemed strange that now as he got well, I fell ill and our roles reversed.

While the rest of the family had days out, Ollie would keep a bedside vigil, not wanting to leave my side. He would hold the bucket while I emptied my already empty stomach, take it to the bathroom and rid its contents, then bring it back, sit, and wait. He placed the cold flannel he had fetched from the bathroom across my brow, murmuring softly, "It'll be all right, Mummy. Don't you worry."

He sat with me for hours. As I drifted in and out of a feverish sleep, he was there. Opening my eyes, I saw him smiling at me. Weak and dehydrated, I could barely lift my arm to hold him, yet he somehow seemed to know and lay down with me, his thin arm light as a feather across my chest as he whispered, "I love you, Mummy, always and forever."

⁓⁓⁓

That summer as we embraced the joy of living and loving, I vowed not to waste a minute. I would truly grasp the wonder of life and its glories, see and appreciate it. I would not take another moment for granted as it whizzed past.

The Universe blessed us that year with many gifts, one of which was a long summer of beautiful, sunshiny skies and perfect temperatures, warm and balmy evenings that allowed us to sit outside and enjoy the wonder of nature.

We had a hammock in our back garden, and Ollie and I spent many timeless moments lying together, enjoying the hum of insects and the sound of trees rustling in tune. One day as we napped, I felt a gentle tug at my sleeve.

"Shhhhh." Ollie nodded toward my chest where a butterfly had landed on his hand. The visitor was dark with bright orange and yellow emblazoned across its gently flapping wings. Ollie remained still, savoring the moment.

"It's beautiful," I said.

"Shhhhh," Ollie repeated, smiling.

I dutifully obliged, and we lay there for a while with this new friend who had come to visit, until Ollie said in a whisper, "Okay, little man, fly away now. Fly away."

The butterfly seemed to ponder this as his wings continued to flap.

Ollie lifted his hand to the skies. "Off you

go now. Off you go." And on cue, it departed my son's hand, hovered, then took flight.

It was not just a moment of beauty, a memory to treasure. It was more. A butterfly starts out as a caterpillar and then picks a spot where he eventually becomes a chrysalis. Then something quite amazing occurs: he is reborn, transformed into a beautiful flying wonder that descends upon the flowers of the earth to pollinate, instill his magic, leave his mark, no matter his short life span.

In Ollie's own way, he was in his own chrysalis while we waited for the glorious rebirth. And when he finally emerged, he would fly like the butterfly, pollinating his love, instilling his magic in all he met.

⁕

The summer of love saw many wonderful moments. Not only did our families stay for several weeks, but we often enjoyed our neighbors' company at the community pool and clubhouse. We shared swimming parties for kids and impromptu barbecues where dads drank too many beers, recalled college years with hearty back slaps, not caring that they'd heard it all before. As the guys jollied, the mums shook their heads in amusement, sipping homemade margaritas. Before too long, the radio would get jacked up as we danced by the pool's edge and our young kids, with hands over their mouths, pretended not to notice and our teens swore they would never do that.

There was a tradition in the community, a kind of inauguration, where children stepped into a new phase in the kid world, cutting the apron strings to become pool warriors. While the pool did have a lifeguard and lessons were offered, there was one thing the lifeguard did not teach. It was a feat all kids in the neighborhood hoped one day to accomplish. They planned for it. They talked about it quietly with their siblings and friends. Fear struck them when mums and dads yelled, "You done it yet, Jimmy? Is today the big day?"

They could often be heard responding, "Not today, Mr. Jones. Tomorrow. I'll do it tomorrow for sure," those apron strings keeping their hold. Kids would learn to swim before they faced the tradition, such was their fear of it.

The cannonball.

When we first arrived in the States, Ollie was five and had spent a summer by the pool with his floaties, not straying too far from his dad or me and playing with his siblings. I can recall how he admired the kids bouncing off the diving board into the deep end, knees tucked under chin, yelling, "Cannonball!"

As they entered the water with a slap, he

laughed at the splash in his face. When Jess and George did it, he cheered loudly and happily yelled, "That will be me soon, you know!"

During the year of his treatment, he had not been able to play in the pool. On days when he was well enough, we would walk him in his buggy to the poolside, where he liked to sit and watch. While his voice was not strong enough for cheering, he would clap softly, then wave, and the kids would yell back at him, "One day, Ollie! One day it will be your turn, little man," and Ollie would smile.

With our extended families, we headed to the pool for the first time that summer and got all the kids sprayed up with sunscreen, quite an accomplishment with six children who had no patience in their excitement to hit the water. We packed our coolers with refreshments, gathered up the assortment of pool toys, and headed off for the afternoon.

The kids eagerly ran out to the pool deck while the mothers in perfect unison yelled after them, "No running by the pool." Setting ourselves up with sun beds and towels, we got busy doing nothing.

My sister got her youngest, Leo, who was three at the time, into his water wings and carried him to the water's edge.

On cue he screamed, not wanting to go in at all.

We all laughed and cajoled him, remembering all of our kids doing the same in years past.

Jess and George were riding their noodles and firing their water guns at some of the older teen girls who didn't like to get their hair wet.

Pete gave them a stern warning, which they ignored with giggles.

Taking in the familiar scenes from typical suburban America like a freeze frame, I smiled as I put Ollie in his float and pulled the straps tighter around his middle.

As I got ready to walk him to the shallow end, he said, "Mummy, I want to do the cannonball."

"What?" I was somewhat surprised. "Are you sure, little man?"

He'd never been in the deep end, not even with his dad or me. He hadn't clung on to us there, like most of the kids had, a kind of prep for the real deal, getting a feel for nothing but water beneath his feet, seeing his toes wriggling in bubbles, maybe even popping his head under the water. It would've been a big deal yet not too bad after all, because he would've been holding on to his mum or dad at the time. It would've been safe.

I was suddenly nervous he hadn't had his prep. Even with his float, he would still go under. He was still terribly frail. What if he slipped off the edge? What if he belly-flopped or did that weird turny thing some kids do when their knees don't tuck properly and they land sideways? I had seen the red welts when this happened and kids got out, putting on a brave face, hiding their pain with a forced grin.

Ollie was adamant. "I want to do the cannon-ball, Mummy. Please?"

"Okay, baby, but only if you let me be in the pool close by. I can catch you if you like."

Ollie rolled his eyes and sighed. "Oh, *okay* then. But you don't need to catch me." He laughed. "I'll be fine."

Ollie was one child we did not need to yell the mantra to. He walked quite slowly, flat footed, an effect of the therapy, and eyed the diving board with awe and glee. Though he was now seven, his frame made him appear much younger. He did not have the strength to pull up his body like the other kids did, so I lifted him onto the board and held his hand.

Ollie's loss of hearing had affected his balance, and vertigo was often an issue. When he let go of my hand, I worried he would fall. A bee buzzed around his head. *Someone on the committee was supposed to have destroyed that bee's nest*, I thought with annoyance.

However, Ollie had something far more important on his mind. "Mummy, aren't you going to get in the pool?"

I did but not before capturing the moment

with the camera and noticing how quiet it had suddenly become around the pool.

All eyes were fixed on Ollie.

I yelled at Pete, who came charging into the center of the pool to join me, and the silence was broken as our family and friends spurred Ollie on.

"Yeah, Ollie!"

"Ollie's going to do the cannonball!"

Others seemed to be thinking, *Oh my God, he's not*, as they glanced in my direction.

I bobbed in the water, waiting for Pete to join me.

Someone turned down the radio, which was playing Katrina and the Waves' "Walking on Sunshine," one of my favorites and weirdly appropriate at that moment.

All eyes were on Ollie.

Gingerly, he walked to the edge.

Thankfully, the bee had gone.

He looked down.

I looked up.

He smiled. With a deep breath, he filled his lungs and at the top of his voice yelled, "Cannonball!"

He jumped.

Thunderous applause and cheers.

With a loud smack, he hit the water, sending out splashes and ripples around the pool.

Kids chanted, "Woohoo!"

"Go, Ollie!"

"Fantastic, Ollie!"

"We knew you could do it!"

With a huge grin, he rose out of the water like King Neptune. Unconcerned about the water up his nose or in his wide joyful eyes, he spluttered and proclaimed his victory. "I did it! I did it! I did the cannonball!" He hugged both his dad and me, adding: "I love you, Mummy and Daddy," with the biggest grin on his cheeky monkey face.

During the entire summer of love, the almost ethereal joy we felt was contagious as our home filled with friends and we celebrated the simple pleasure of being together, watching the kids play, and drinking wine until merry.

Pete was on vacation while our families stayed for almost two months. With time of no consequence, we let the kids stay up late and have sleepovers, and we enjoyed lazy Sunday mornings seven days a week.

Living in a constant state of euphoria, Pete and I drew closer. If ever there was a time to reconnect, this was certainly it, but I wondered if it would be enough.

Top: Ollie, 4 months old.

Bottom left: "Hey, Mum!" First bike, 3 years old.

Bottom right: Playing in the back garden.

Top: Day at the mall
    with Mum.

Bottom left: Love that cheeky monkey grin!

Bottom right: George and Ollie, brothers forever,
    enjoying the funfair.

Top: It's cannonball time! Summer of love, 2003

Bottom left: George and Ollie at the beach with Daddy.

Bottom right: "Let's build a castle!" Fun times in
Walberswick.

Top: Off to school for art day. A good day.

Bottom: Birthday boy!

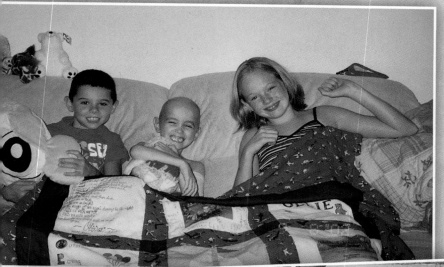

Top: Jess, George, and Ollie snuggled in the quilt our friends created with love. One of my favorite pictures of my children.

Bottom: A bike ride around the house.
"Lead the way, Ollie!"

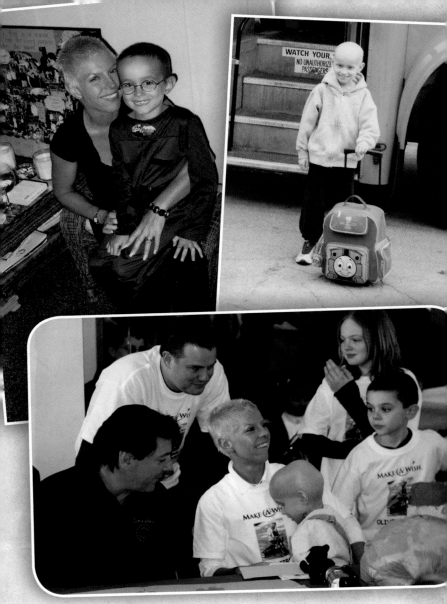

Top left: A carefree evening during the summer of love,
2003. His new hair was so soft!

Top right: "School day, and I'm so ready!"

Bottom: Wish Day at Downers Grove station along
with David Hood.

Top: An exhausted yet
     happy Ollie after
     driving the Metra
     train on Wish Day.

Bottom: Wish Ball with Peter, Jess, and George.
        Metra Chairman Jeffrey Ladd announces the
        release of Engine 401 into service and makes
        Ollie's true dream a reality.

Ollie's bike.

CHAPTER 12
The Truth

I remember my first crush. I was nine, and her name was Lily. She had the bluest eyes I had ever seen and a giggle to melt even the toughest heart. I loved everything about Lily. The way she twirled her hair around her pinkie, how cute she looked in her favorite red polka-dot dress, how incredibly long her eyelashes were, how soft her skin looked, and how she *smelt*: fresh and warm, like a spring day. Being around her made my heart sing. I never questioned the crush, did not think it odd; it was just my heart going where it wanted to go.

I liked boys. They were fun to hang with, and I felt comfortable around them. I was kind of tomboyish and liked being outdoors more than in. I rode my bike down to the woods at the end of the street, went tree climbing, and as a teenager smoked my first cigarette stolen from Mum's pack—all with the boys.

It was only when Tommy, my next-door neighbor and friend, tried to kiss me that I positively cringed and began to wonder.

Tommy was the boy all of the girls wanted and chatted about constantly. He was tall for his fourteen years and had long, dark, curly hair, brown eyes that looked almost black, and a mole on his left cheek that the girls would swear was a beauty spot. He was gorgeous.

Jemma, one of the few girls with whom I did hang out, had the biggest crush on him. When I told her what had happened, she was insanely jealous and couldn't understand why I didn't like him.

"But I do like him," I said. "Just, well, he's just not my type, that's all."

Jemma was bewildered.

It was true; I did like Tommy. He was my friend.

Yet I knew there was more to it than that. I knew because if I imagined Tommy's older sister kissing me, I got an altogether different feeling and a stirring inside of me that wouldn't go away.

As I grew older, my sister and I would talk about the men we would marry and how many kids we'd have, all the typical sisterly stuff. I so wanted to share with her how I was feeling, but I thought she would think me weird.

Our upbringing was a strict one, and my mum struggled raising four kids alone for a time. Being the eldest, I was expected to help out. I had daily chores, even on the weekends, and Mum ruled the house with a discipline that was sometimes scary. My sister was the youngest and often played that up to Mum, who doted on her.

The truth was I was scared to tell my sister also because I feared she would tell Mum, who'd send me off to some reform school for not being normal.

This is what happened to my twin brother, Stephen, when he was seventeen. For him it was not some special school but the British army, a place where a lot of parents sent their young sons who either had poor grades that would not be enough for them to find a decent job or who had a problem of some sort. "Send them to the army. That will sort 'em out," they'd say.

Ironically, my openly gay brother, Steve, had an absolute blast in the army and actually met his first love there. He was and is a great patriot, loved the monarchy, fully embraced the military as a Grenadier Guard, and served for many years. He even enjoyed visits to Buckingham Palace, where he would stand on sentry duty in all his glory as visitors took pictures and tried to make him talk or laugh, which when guarding Her Majesty is not the done thing.

When we were kids growing up in rural England, people didn't openly discuss certain things, such as emotions and feelings. It would be years before some family members and most of the local community would accept my brother's orientation.

Although I admired his bravery, I did not have his courage and kept my own feelings hidden.

Though I knew I was not attracted to men, I knew I wanted children. I wanted to feel what it was like to carry a child and wondered if I ever would. The sadness of that not happening furthered my anxieties.

As years passed, I became a fantastic actress. I tried to convince myself that I could have a boyfriend. After all, this is what was expected of me, what was supposed to happen, and I didn't want to let my family down.

I began a flip-flopping of sorts, dating boys and taking them home to meet the family. Mum would declare enthusiastically, "Well, he's just lovely, Deborah. My, oh my, so handsome! My goodness, he's in the Royal Air Force." The thought of grandchildren bouncing on her knee delighted her, and who was I to take that away?

At the same time I was dating men, I had a secret. As the only member of my family who knew, my brother, Steve, was able to guide me to places where I could meet other women like me.

During my years of dating men, my family never questioned why somehow or other it just didn't work out.

So the charade continued, until something unexpected happened.

A group of girlfriends from work asked me to go out to a club.

At first I said, "No, I'm tired from work, so you guys go without me. I'm having an early night."

Well, they badgered me until reluctantly I agreed.

Halfheartedly I dressed and made my way to the club where I'd meet up with the girls.

The first thing I noticed was that he was pretty. His brown hair with hints of blond was swept back like John Travolta's in *Saturday Night Fever*, and his smile made his whole face glow. He was propped up at the bar, talking to some girls who gazed up at him admiringly, though he looked like he couldn't care less about them. About six feet tall, he was skinny in lean pants and a tight shirt and looked as if he had just stepped off the catwalk.

I found myself staring at his crotch. Quickly I

averted my eyes, yet he had already seen me. Worse, he had seen me *looking*.

He grinned.

I walked toward the table where my coworkers sat and said, "Who's that?"

"Oh, that's Peter. Peter Tibbles. Isn't he adorable?"

Later that night I asked him to dance. In the coming weeks, I found myself falling in love. Passionately, hopelessly, recklessly, magically *in love*.

I took him to meet my parents and was no longer acting when I proudly showed off my new beau. I relished meeting his family and joyfully became a part of it.

As I happily looked into his eyes, I saw my children waiting to be born. Putting my previous life to bed, I imagined it had never happened. Almost. I felt so passionately for this man that I thought my old feelings must have been some phase. They had to be, right?

Pete's and my love would stay a long time. We got married and had our children. I threw myself into motherhood, this new kind of love, this love like no other. I became the happy suburban mum who took my husband and my life for granted and imagined there would always be this joy.

But now with cancer on board and all that had happened, I was questioning again. As I observed

the courage of our child, from treatments to can-
nonballs, the shame of past lies and of being fake
haunted me.

As the rewind button played out memories in
my head, I wondered what would happen to Pete
and me. Could we press the play button together? I
knew Pete was hoping we could.

The joy of just living as our child embraced
each day, showering us all with the preciousness of
life, instilled in both of us the possibility.

For me, that was enough.

Our families prepared to return to England armed
with memories of a lifetime: days by the pool, barbecues, Chuck E. Cheese's, Brookfield Zoo, tripping over train tracks, laughing at Granddad with
his big ears. They tenderly packed away handmade
cards made of glitter and glue with the words *I
love you*. We'd found forgotten home movies and
one in particular of a time spent in Walberswick,
home to Grandma and Granddad, which we had
fondly named Wobbly Wick.

Walberswick is a rural, unchanged, historical village in Britain with century-old traditions, such
as gentlemen tipping their hats to you as you pass
them in the street. It is a place where everyone

knows your name, where people gather daily at the local pub to down a pint and exchange local gossip, and where a chap on his bike delivers groceries to your door. It is a wonderful retreat from the hustle and bustle of living in London.

The video had been shot while I enjoyed a weekend at my sister's home and Pete took the kids to Walberswick to enjoy some quality time with their grandparents. They went kite flying, one of their favorite pastimes.

Kites flew high in the sky on that blustery day. With yelps of delight, the kids ran freely across the hilly sand dunes.

In the background, Pete hollered encouragement. "Good job, George! That's it; keep a tight hold on that line."

The camera then cut to a scene where he was sitting in the sand with Ollie nestled between his legs. All we could see in the video was the bottom halves of Ollie's and Pete's legs as Pete held the camera above, looking down.

"Are you tired, little man?" Pete said. "Are you ready to head back to Grandma and Granddad's?"

Ollie's arms and hands snuggled closer to his dad. "No, not yet, Daddy. I want to stay here with you a little bit longer. I love you, Daddy."

"Okay, little man. I love you too."

Then only the wind in the background could be heard, time of no significance as the loving silence was captured forever.

We watched other home movies from past Christmases to feeding the squirrels at Greenwich Park. We laughed at Jessica's tantrum when one of the boys gave food to *her* squirrel and she kicked the stroller to the ground and stomped off, nose in the air.

Along with the replayed memories and all the family activity during these months, we had moments when nothing happened. Those were the greatest of all.

I didn't want it to end and nervously wondered as summer drew to a close what fall would bring.

～～♡♡～～

With the school year approaching, the kids prepared excitedly. As always, we took them to school to check out their new classes and to find out which classmates would be joining them.

Kids from all grades along with their parents clamored at the entrance doors checking out the class lists posted on the door. As Ollie approached, the throng of kids began waving and cheering, "Welcome back, Ollie!" The sea of children parted, creating a pathway for Ollie to make his way forward.

Smiling shyly, Ollie gave high fives to the kids as some patted him on the back. There were parents, some of whom I didn't even know, who nodded and smiled in my direction. Others voiced their welcome: "Hey, Ollie! How ya doin'? You look so great. It's so good to see you," or "Nice to have you back, Oliver. You look wonderful. Looking forward to school, bud?"

Ollie smiled. "Yes, I can't wait!"

The school routine began the way it always had: Marmite on toast or scrambled eggs, rucksacks at the ready. With the second episode of *Arthur* at an end, the boys left for the bus stop on the corner, mere yards from our house.

The only difference this year would be that Jess would stand on the opposite side of the street waiting for a different bus to take her to Jefferson Junior High School.

She finished preening herself after I yelled upstairs for the umpteenth time, "Jess, come on. You're gonna miss your bus."

Breathless, she appeared at the top of the stairs and asked, "Does this look okay, or do you think the white top looks better?" She twirled on the spot like a catwalk model.

In my head, I said, *Oh, for goodness' sake.* What I said was, "I think that looks great, Jess. You'll knock 'em dead! Now come on."

As my children waited for their buses, I watched from the window. I'd promised the boys that when their bus came, I would come out to the front porch as always and wave to them until the bus disappeared.

On the corner of the bus stop was a large rock with a fairly smooth surface, so smooth you could sit on it. It's the site of two more traditions among the Prentiss Creek neighborhood kids. A few feet away from the rock was a tree. Historically, all kids who stood at that bus stop through grade school had climbed that tree and stood tall on the rock. All except Ollie.

As I observed Jess with her new school outfit, rucksack, and hairdo, I smiled. I knew she would have a fantastic day. My gaze crossed the street to my boys. George stood on the rock, his rucksack thrown haphazardly against the tree. Looking up in adoration of his big brother, Ollie stood on the ground below.

Nearby other kids played a game of tag, a bit of rough and tumble on the ground, knees already scraped. Girls chatted incessantly, oblivious to the relevance of what was about to happen.

With tears in my eyes and several deep breaths that caught me completely unaware, I watched my eldest son take his younger brother's hand and pull him up on the rock. Side by side, they stood tall, Ollie wearing the biggest, proudest grin I'd ever seen.

A few days later, George helped his little brother complete one more Prentiss Creek tradition, and I was the only parent who did not yell at her child, "Get down off that tree!"

With school in full swing we settled back into the routine of homework, after-school activities, and spending time with new friends. Nobody pursued this with more zest than Ollie.

Though no longer on therapy, Ollie still bore the scars, one of which was the short-term memory loss typical of medulloblastoma. For example, if I asked Ollie to go to the refrigerator to take out milk, butter, and eggs, he would forget the butter. As a result of this memory loss, Ollie had to work a bit harder in school.

I had met with the principal prior to school resuming to discuss Ollie's future education, and it was decided he would still get the support of his school aides. Extra tuition help for home was also offered should we need it.

The school's support was tireless. To combat his learning issues, everything would have to be written down and repeated, repeated, repeated. Where once upon a time he would only need to study about ten minutes for a ten-word spelling test, he would now have to spend an hour or so. No matter how tired he got, he persisted and never once complained.

Stew told me once about a patient of his who had the same difficulties but overcame them with the help of his family and the school district. This patient not only graduated with honors but went on to university and now helped children facing the same challenges to take each step up the ladder of academic life, giving them hope for the future, no matter what adversity they faced.

I loved the way Stew reflected on how these adversities affected a child. I appreciated the simplicity of how he put it. "Well, Deb, if Ollie was an A student before cancer, it just means he'll be a B or C student," he said with a smile.

Truth be told, high grades didn't seem that important anymore.

Ollie's medical care would be ongoing, and he would need MRIs for the next ten to fifteen years to keep an eye on possible regrowth. Organ function would still need to be checked, and he was definitely going to need a hearing aid. I made a mental note to set an appointment for it.

Ollie's first six-week MRI was due. We were anxious, of course, yet not overly worried. He was full of energy and doing so well, loving every minute of school, looking forward to Halloween.

Meanwhile, I positively sang and danced my way into my own class each day.

The summer of love had followed us into fall, and we were full of hope.

CHAPTER 13
The Big Dipper

Remember the feeling, the thrill, of losing your stomach as you hurtled down a roller coaster? As adults we have a tendency to always look on the worst side of things. We imagine screws coming loose. We think about the appearance of that maintenance guy—disheveled, like he'd been up all night, cursing under his breath, out of sorts—and with fear in our stomachs we wonder if he made those safety checks. Yet for kids the feeling is pure exhilaration. Implicitly trusting, they scream joyfully, "Again! Let's go again!"

Not far from where I grew up in England was a place called Dreamland, an old, worn-out fair complete with bumper cars, merry-go-round, and a hall of mirrors scarier than the dilapidated ghost ride. Teen boys who ran the show strutted along the tracks like James Dean, cigarettes hanging loosely from their lips, while girls giggled.

The crème de la crème, the star of the show, was the old wooden Big Dipper. Losing your stomach was where it was at.

The only other attraction to provide a similar thrill was The Waltzer, where those same pubescent boys would select cars of certain lucky girls to stand on as it threw them around in circles. The problem with The Waltzer was that you had to hold on to your stomach and the contents in it. I usually gave The Waltzer a wide berth, the mere thought of it making me want to throw up.

In the late fall after the summer of love, my stomach dipped with a huge whoosh when I received a phone call from the school secretary. I barely heard Missy's apologetic words as I went crashing down, down. Suddenly I was back at The Waltzer, holding on for dear life, but the neon sign didn't read Dreamland. It flashed grotesquely Headache.

"Mrs. Tibbles?" The voice on the other end of the line brought me back to reality.

"I'm sorry," I stammered. "Yes. Okay, I'll come get him."

I stood for a moment, remembering the Sundays Dad would have a custody visit and off we'd go, singing, "Ten green bottles . . ." or "There was an old lady who swallowed a fly. I don't know why she swallowed the fly. Perhaps she'll die. She swallowed the fly to catch the spider that wriggled and tickled and wriggled inside her. Perhaps she'll die." We would never tire of those songs, no matter how many times we sang them.

I stood in Dreamland, remembering holding Dad's hand, looking up in awe at the Big Dipper while my other hand held candy floss, my mouth in sticky glee. Not once did I fear the Big Dipper. It was powerful and took me on a magical ride outside my often traumatic childhood. It held promise.

I pulled myself together and drove to the school, the radio blasting a random song that kept the tears away.

I entered the sick bay.

Missy gave me a pitiful smile.

Ollie lay clutching his head, weeping.

Someone had hit the rewind button of my life.

The Waltzer whooshed, and I held on.

⁘

At home, I gave Ollie meds and lay with him on the couch. Knowing he would sleep for hours, I moved him to his bed and walked downstairs.

Standing at the kitchen sink, I looked out the window at the swaying swing. Taking a breath, I made my way to the pantry where I stocked cans, wrapping paper, bags, and general bits and bobs. It was here that I had put away the baby intercom back in early June. I retrieved it and the extension for the outlet, went upstairs, and quietly plugged it in.

I sat on the edge of Ollie's bed and observed him sleeping. So peaceful. So *healthy*. Gazing at my beautiful child, I did not mourn for me but allowed the anger to settle for him. He would never be afforded so much of life, but he was more deserving than anyone I knew. Strangely the outrage empowered me to make a new silent promise. One I would move heaven and earth for. One I would risk my marriage—anything and everything— for. It was the one thing that mattered.

He would not suffer again.

He would board the Big Dipper that was so powerful, that held so much promise. He would yelp joyfully and ride to a magical world where anything is possible and nothing changes, where beauty, joy, and peace are eternal.

All I had to do was convince Pete, who I imagined wasn't aware of the Big Dipper.

The next day Ollie woke bright and early, as he always did. From the kitchen, I heard him quietly come down the stairs. I knew what he was about to do. Standing at the kitchen sink and looking out the window to our back garden, I hummed a tune. As he tiptoed into the kitchen, I could picture his grin.

Suddenly he yelled, "Boo! Gotcha!"

As he grabbed my waist, I pretended to jump out of my skin. "Oh! You made me jump, you cheeky monkey." I picked up my giggling boy and swung him around.

The previous day's episode clearly forgotten, he was full of beans.

"So, want some breakfast, little man?"

Nodding, he said, "I think I will have scrambled eggs today, Mummy, please, and can I have some ketchup too?"

Putting him back down on the floor, I said, "Well, of course you can, and I'll get you some juice too, okay?"

"Okay, Mummy." He walked to the family room, where he turned on the TV and settled down to watch *Clifford the Big Red Dog*.

I could hear Jess and George stirring upstairs

as I made breakfast.

Thinking about what had happened the previous day, I wondered what I would do next. I first needed to talk to Stew.

After I waved the kids off to school, I picked up the phone and told Stew what had happened.

I swear I could sense his heart sinking as he solemnly said, "Okay, let's get an MRI done so we can see where we're at. How's he doin' today?"

I replied truthfully, "Oh, he's absolutely fine today, you know. Completely back to normal, and he's gone off to school, but—" I faltered for a moment. "Well, you know, Stew, I just have this feeling. I wish I didn't."

Stew paused and with softness in his voice said, "I gotta tell ya. Your instinct has always been right. I wish it weren't the case, but my gut tells me the same. Let me get an MRI appointment set up, and then we'll have you guys in to chat some more, okay?"

I whispered, "Yes," and hung up.

Immediately I called my sister Kaz in England. Not wanting to make small talk at all, I just blurted out, "Kaz, it's Ollie. It's back."

What could she say, really? One minute she was probably yelling at the kids to stop jumping on the furniture while she got dinner ready, thinking, *Oh, I really must go and collect my jacket from the dry cleaners,* when suddenly the phone rang, her sister sounding a bit strange and saying her nephew was sick again. Only she must have known this was not about being sick. What could she have said, except sorry, which must have seemed trivial when the full horror of what was being said hung in the air because she *knew*. So she said something else that meant so much more: "I love you, Deb."

And then we cried.

Pete was devastated, yet still he clung to hope. He told me about some healing facility in Los Angeles where people apparently healed others simply by placing their hands across a person.

I wanted to laugh and cry at the same time. Part of me wanted to go, yet the minute I thought that, a voice inside whispered, *No.* Would Pete think that voice was as nuts as I thought the healing hands were?

I let out a hysterical laugh as I imagined the conversation, or rather fight, we'd have about the voice and healing hands.

I knew the voice was not nuts.

I knew he was desperate.

I wished he could hear the voice.

We agreed to wait until after the MRI to speak to our children and our families, wanting to savor the lingering happiness.

That night I ran a bath for Ollie. Jess was in her room chatting to friends on her cell phone while Ollie and George played in the family room, building up the train set and giggling at the antics of the conductor played by Alec Baldwin in *The Magic Railroad*, one of Ollie's favorite movies.

I called, "Ollie! Bath is ready. Come on up, little man."

I heard him tell George to leave the trains where they were till he got back and make his way up the stairs. He called, "Do you have all the toys in the tub I like?"

"Of course!"

As he undressed, I tested the water again to make sure it was not too hot.

Once in the tub, he played with his favorite assortment of cars and trains, his shark with a half-eaten man in its mouth, and his rubber duck. He played with his numerous syringes, old heparin and saline flushes that were just perfect for water guns. He lathered all around his head and face and pretended to be Santa, then used his makeshift water guns to squirt me, the ceiling, and just about everywhere else.

Out of nowhere he said, "Mummy? I'm sick again, aren't I?"

I was completely caught unaware.

His big brown eyes looked at me, and his hands rested gently on his knees as toys floated around the tub.

Desperately I wished to not say what I knew I must. I knelt in front of him and stroked his cheek, noticing the bubbles lingering on his head. "Yes, baby," I replied, "there is some tumor growing again."

A pause. "Do I have to have a line put back in?"

I kissed his nose, hating the conversation. His nakedness, his innocence, was heartrending. I noticed his tiny penis bobbing in the water, and pain stabbed at me. There would be no children for this child, no nothing, just this bathtub with toys.

I fought the compulsion to get in and hold him and willed the stinging tears away.

"You still feel pretty good right now, don't you, little man?"

He nodded. "Except I am tired, and I felt funny today. Will I have to go back on the magic table? I don't want to go back on the magic table." Tears rolled slowly down his cheeks and into the bubbles.

"I know you don't, sweetie, and I want you to know that we're not going to do anything you don't want, okay, little man?"

Ollie listened intently.

"I love you, baby. You've been such a brave,

strong boy, and we're all so proud of you. Whatever you want is what we want, okay? If you say to me, 'Mummy, I'm done. I don't want any more therapy,' then we will not do any more. If you want to try just one more time, then that is also okay, sweetie."

He nodded sadly. "Will I get sick again if we do more?"

I told him truthfully what Stew had said: that these new therapies were not as severe in their side effects but would still have some impact nonetheless. I did not tell him that his body would probably not be able to endure any more toxicity. I did not tell him what I felt. It was important to me that he make the choice or, at the least, have some say in the final decision.

His tears continued to fall as he considered what he wanted.

I really don't recall how long those moments of thought lasted, but his tears were gone when he dove his shark deep into the water, looked up, and said, "I think I will try just one more time."

As simple as that, I found myself brightly saying, "Okay, good. I'll call Stew and let him know. You are due for an MRI, so we can get the line put back in while we're there."

In typical Ollie form, he grinned and said, "Oh, goody! I get to see all my nurses and play in the playroom again."

Ollie's wise old soul had spoken.

I was certain he had come to this choice not for himself but for his family, in particular for his dad, who was positively ecstatic when I told him. I'd have to wait to introduce him to the Big Dipper.

Two days later we were sitting with Stew, looking at images of growth, while our son was in surgery getting a new line. The mood was somber as Stew gave us all the options, including stem cell transplant, only to rule it out when we realized the risk: Ollie was unlikely to survive the transplant after toxic shock. The latest trial therapies, so new only a handful of statistics existed, were his only hope.

"Of course, this has to be your decision," Stew said. "I can give you all the options, quote statistics, offer some advice, but at the end of the day you have to sit down and decide what is truly best for Ollie. When many parents reach this point, they want to afford their child some quality time, and I understand that. I want to stress to you guys right now, he will not suffer any pain. We have some pretty strong stuff that can take care of everything, I promise you."

Looking at Pete he compassionately continued.

"I also see and understand that you would want to do all you can to save your son. My God, that's only natural, and if you guys decide to try some research therapy, we'll put him on a trial best suited to him medically. But this decision, as difficult as it is, has to be your own. I can't make it for you."

We sat in silence, time unimportant.

I continued to wipe away the annoying tears that would not stop coming.

Momentarily, I remembered Great Ormond Street Hospital and the horror of what they told us as we sat there not fully comprehending such devastating news. We had come so far on this journey. Ollie had fought so hard. I imagined him lying on the table, Ticky close by, and thought again of his decision, of his selfless love, of his always putting others before himself.

I thought of the Big Dipper and reached for Pete's hand. Squeezing it, I prayed he would allow his son a fantastic ride out and knew the time had come to tell him so.

Sitting in that room as we discussed our son, knowing he would die eventually even if Pete wasn't ready to admit it, I was amazingly calm despite the tears. I felt so different than I had at Great Ormond Street. I didn't even feel anger. All I wanted to do was get on so that I could get back home to our children, our friends, to our cat Ella, and to *living*.

Ollie had said he wanted to try, and he had declared with a smile how much he looked forward to seeing those wonderful nurses and the playroom again. Suddenly I got it. This *was* his life. Ollie had struggled, endured, almost died, yet through all those times under the care of this amazing man and the staff at Children's Memorial, my son had remained happy. His life *was* Stew and Children's Memorial Hospital.

For Ollie, coming here was like coming home. To return, like a wounded soldier after years of battle, was a homecoming of sorts, with banners waving and crowds cheering, giving Ollie a warm, happy, safe feeling. How appropriate he should live out his final months or weeks in both of his homes where he was loved unconditionally.

After discussing all the trial therapies open to us, we agreed to start the phase two trial of Oxaliplatin, the trial believed to be best suited to Ollie.

While Pete desperately hoped this would be the miraculous drug that would cure our son, Stew told us honestly what we could expect: "If Ollie responds well to this, then what I hope we see is a delay in growth, in spread, so that we can prolong his life a little more." Sensitively aware of our feelings and concerns, he smiled kindly and went on. "You know, I've been amazed many a time. You just never know."

His words fed the hope Pete clung to.

Pete and I agreed on two issues. First, if the next MRI revealed progress had been made, we would continue with therapy, but if further spread occurred, we would stop the therapy. Second, we would tell Jess and George some new tumor had been found and Ollie would be resuming therapy. We would say nothing else unless they asked *that* question.

Like many parents, we were blinded to the insight of children, that they see, hear, and feel everything. They asked.

With Ollie looking so well, it was easier in a way. Ironically, it was Ollie who gave Jess and George hope because his physical appearance didn't reveal what was happening inside. They seemed to look at him and think, *Well, he has a chance. I mean, look at how good he looks.*

They were amazingly calm as they asked about side effects. Would his hair fall out again? Would he be in the hospital a lot again? Would the therapy work?

We responded truthfully with what Stew had told us. "Yes, he will lose his hair again and, yes, he may be in hospital again." A pause. "Yes, there is a *chance*, but it's slim, that he may not respond."

They listened and questioned, the weight of it all sinking in.

"Is he going to die?" Jessica said.

Shoulders heavy, her dad sighed. "We don't know. We are hoping this therapy is the one."

"We are hopeful, of course," I said. "It was Ollie who said he wanted to try one last time. Yet the chances, to be honest, are not good." A stifling pause. "And, yes, he is probably going to die."

There. I had said it. I'd had to. I knew Pete couldn't.

I felt like I was out of my body, looking down on a scene from a Lifetime Original Movie. Any minute now we would all have a family hug. We'd wipe away tears and take a commanding stance of love, strength, and hope with Pete as our fearless leader. Violins would play in the background.

Our brutal reality was a broken father slumped in a chair, a deafening silence, and our children looking at us with lost, empty eyes.

Out of the silence, I heard Ollie humming a tune while he played in the family room. What a godsend his hearing loss was.

I sensed the kids wanted to leave the room, yet they stayed. I was reminded of their table manners. Sitting at the kitchen table after eating, the kids would usually say politely, "Can I get down from the table, please?" Other times, when perhaps a friend was over, their excitement sent table manners flying out the window as they wolfed down food and leapt from the table. Then we would shake our heads in a way that was meant to appear disapproving yet never was.

They wanted to leave, only this time they wanted our permission, wanted us to give the order. To me, it seemed they felt their leaving such a terrible conversation or even asking to leave would demonstrate an ugly irreverence.

I was about to give the command when Ollie walked in, hands on hips.

"So there you all are. I was wondering where you'd gone. Are we going to watch this movie or what?" he said rather cheekily.

Though tears welled in their eyes, Jessica and George laughed.

We all laughed, grateful for his wonderful intrusion at precisely the right moment.

"Yeah, let's watch the movie," said Jess and George.

I smiled at them.

Suddenly seeming so much older, they smiled back.

Then Pete rose from his chair and scooped

up Ollie. Like a firefighter, he threw him over his shoulder, then tickled him as he ran around the house yelling, "Oooaargh." He sounded ridiculously like a pirate, and we laughed while Ollie squealed his delight and rained down pretend punches on his daddy's back.

I walked toward Jess and George and gave them hugs, kissing each of them on the forehead. "I love you," I said, hugging them closer.

They held me tight.

"Want some popcorn?" I said.

They nodded and followed me into the kitchen, giggling at Ella, who was crouched under the table, hiding from the crazy firefighter who sounded like a pirate.

The Lifetime Original Movie was playing after all.

CHAPTER 14
All of You

Our journey continued, and we were acutely aware we were nearing a destination we'd hoped we'd never reach. Ollie's therapy had no impact. The tumors were growing at an alarming rate. Seeing the snakelike growth in his brain and spine, we instantly understood why this cancer, medulloblastoma, was named after Medusa, the Greek goddess whose once beautiful tresses became hideous snakes and whose stare could turn men into stone. How could something so evil live in my child, whose love shone so brightly it bathed everyone in love?

I had read the book *Tuesdays with Morrie* by Mitch Albom, which truthfully and compassionately chronicles the author's college professor Morrie's impending death. Aware of life's beauty, Morrie was unafraid to leave this world. I wanted to know how my child felt. My greatest fear, which I battled daily, was that Ollie was scared. I wondered, *Do I ask him? What do I say?*

I did not ask. I allowed fear to get the better of me. What would I say if he told me he was scared to die? Or that he knew he was dying and didn't want to? What if he *pleaded* with me for his very *life*, which I, his mother, his *protector*, could not save? I couldn't fathom such a horrendous conversation. I knew I would not be able to comfort him and say, "Don't worry, my child. Mummy will take care of you." How could I when buried deep within was the feeling that I had failed him?

When we knew the appalling truth and Stew told us to take our child home, there was a stifling serenity, a strange calmness that was almost suffocating, at least for me.

My husband preferred the horrible silence of the grief already present. He could not speak of it, turning instead to the comfort in a bottle, quenching his pain with a liquid that threatened to destroy him.

When he was with our children, he was back in that Lifetime Original Movie. He would play, take them out, and relish the precious moments of doing nothing. He would lie with them on the couch and linger there.

But once they were safely tucked up in bed, it became too much for him, another day over, another day closer, and he'd open a second bottle of red wine.

There never was a moment when we told Ollie he was done with treatment for good, and he did not question why we were stopping it.

When we told him this round was over, he said, "Thank goodness for that. I love you."

I knew that he *knew*, and I despised myself for not having the courage to ask him the question that plagued me.

Ollie's pain relief came via a button he would press whenever he needed it. I noticed the supply diminishing between each fusion every twenty-four hours. Sometimes he would fall asleep and awaken in pain. He never screamed or complained, yet I could see it etched in his beautiful face.

He was also on steroids to combat the seizures, which were so small we barely noticed them but were becoming more frequent.

One day I walked into the living room, where

Ollie had been eating a sandwich. He was slumped to the right, his sandwich still in his hand, and Jess was wiping the drool from his mouth. She tenderly put him back into an upright position. Slowly he came around, confused as if waking from a nap, and continued to eat as though nothing had happened.

Jess understood. She *knew*, as did George.

We did not speak of it.

We dealt with the waiting, the knowing. We smiled, even laughed, in the face of death.

We did all this because of love, which had the power to override *everything*. We didn't want to waste a moment. All of us were suffering deep inside—my husband, the kids, and I—yet we put that aside because what was more important was time with Ollie, sharing our love, enjoying each minute that cruelly ticked past.

We could smile and laugh because being in his presence was a gift, and while unwrapping that gift we found layer upon layer of the joys of life that we'd once taken for granted. Each time the gift presented itself differently and in many ways soothed our weeping souls. We were losing him, yet he was healing us, preparing us. *Saving* us.

These weeks were some of our happiest.

During the Christmas season of 2003, Pete's parents joined us. Of course, they spoiled not just Ollie but all the kids. We decorated the house with over-the-top, gaudy decorations, hung lights in each room, and played worn-out Christmas songs that we never tired of. It was a glorious time.

I was particularly happy for Pete, hoping that perhaps he could share some of his darkest thoughts with his parents, yet I realized it was equally too much for them. They were losing their grandson and knew this was the last time they would see him. I accepted that their being there was enough for Pete.

On Christmas morning, Pete's dad, Brian, rose early, donned the Santa hat, and conducted a family tradition he had passed to his son. While a crackly Jim Reeves album played loudly, he entered the kids' room and yelled like a child, "He's been. He's been!"

The kids bounced out of their beds to see what goodies were in the overflowing stockings at the ends of their beds.

The tradition of Christmas would continue

with a light breakfast, leaving room for the sweeties, of course. The adults corked the champagne and got busy for the feast to be served midafternoon.

With the day in full swing, the phone was hot with calls to family in England. The kids got high on chocolate, and drinking champers put a glow on our cheeks. We played silly games, watched movies, and created our own.

Granddad gave Ollie a horsey ride on his back while I called out, "Be careful!"

Ollie frowned at me and called, "Giddyup, Granddad!"

The day after Christmas, Boxing Day in England, a national holiday also observed in Australia and Canada, is an annual excuse to party. True to form, we did just that. Leftovers of cold turkey accompanied cauliflower cheese, baked potato, and anything with pickles and cheese, most popular being Branston Pickle, which we ate with just about everything, and of course Marmite sarnies.

While we spend Christmas Day with immediate family only, on Boxing Day we invite the rest of the clan along with friends. Much merrymaking ensues. That year, we opened up our home to all who wanted to attend.

No one would have guessed Ollie's weakening state.

Each in turn, friends gathered him up and danced with him in our dining room–turned–makeshift disco with flashing lights and loud music. Twirling him round and round as he giggled, everyone failed to notice the medical supplies still lining the walls and the IV pole disguised as a Christmas tree in the corner.

Christmas came and went with good-byes to grandparents, but Pete had a surprise in store.

Pete astonished us all with a trip to Disney World. We saw in the New Year at the Animal Kingdom in a beautiful log cabin nestled in a wood where we could see the Magic Kingdom from the deck. It was a perfect location, quiet and peaceful so Ollie could rest when he needed yet with the hustle and bustle of a fairyland a boat ride away. As night fell on New Year's Eve, the sky burst alive with a fireworks display.

For years we had talked about taking the kids to Disney World and scoffed at it as too expensive and a waste of time. Now it was neither.

The money we didn't have was well spent as we treasured the time together on silly rides, painting our faces, and meeting favorite characters, all of which the kids recorded in their special autograph books.

Pete and I took turns staying at the cabin on days it was too much for Ollie, while the other would take Jess and George out.

We also visited Universal Studios and Sea World. Ollie's favorite part was visiting the faux set of *Jaws*, one of his favorite movies. I half expected him to sing the song from the movie like we used to, "Show me the way to go home. I'm tired, and I want to go to bed," then squeeze his paper cup, mirroring the famous scene in the movie and making us laugh.

We didn't want our trip to end. It was booked for a week, yet Pete extended it.

By mid-January, it was time to go home.

The kids got back into the swing of school. Ollie went on days he felt like it, sometimes just for an hour or so and usually on Friday, art day, his favorite and a reason to save his energy.

If not attending school, he would spend time on the couch with his other favorite pastime, card making. He would make cards for everyone: family, friends, nurses, teachers, and anyone he loved, which meant he was always making those cards.

They were all similar. Little stickers of animals; trains; SpongeBob; big, red felt-tip hearts with glitter and the words *Love, Love, Love* and *I Love You* aplenty.

One day his favorite teacher, Mrs. S., who was also his school aide, told me of something that Ollie had given to her over a period of several days. Each day he would hand her an envelope, and inside was a single piece of a puzzle. Eventually, she had been given all the pieces, yet she could not figure this puzzle out and was quite frustrated. She did not dare to ask Ollie and turned instead to her own daughter, who was a little older than Ollie, who put the puzzle together in no time. It turned out to be an elephant, which she thought was endearing. However, her daughter said, "Turn it over, Mom." As she did, she saw in Ollie's child-like scribble, *I love you.*

The messages from Ollie, whether in a card, a word, or a look, afforded an awareness of *truth.* I was learning. We all were. I could sense change in us all, a quiet reflection and humility. We were looking out to the world and realizing so much of it was trivial and unimportant.

We were aware we were fragile. That life was fragile and not to be wasted. That we shouldn't sweat the small stuff. That we must live the life we want, not the one others imagine we should. That we must live honestly, with kindness, and be happy.

Once again I found myself wondering whether my marriage would survive. Did I want it to? I questioned who I was. Focusing on the pain, the shock it would cause my family, I found myself avoiding what I already suspected.

On a good day, Ollie would have a play date. One such time, he asked if he could sleep over.

I panicked at first, my thoughts focused on the worst. What if? Strangely, the horrible thought was quickly answered by a voice in my head. *It will be fine.* I was getting accustomed to these feelings, these comforting words that came and were always right.

The hardest part was explaining it to Pete, who was not at all comfortable with Ollie going.

"But he'll be fine, Pete. I just know it."

An incredulous Pete eventually gave in after he realized how fun it would be for Ollie and when he was reassured we would be in constant contact. After all, he was only a few houses down the road. We could be there in a flash if we had to.

Ollie took great joy in packing his overnight bag of projects and goodies and was in high spirits when I dropped him off. I knew he would have a blast.

Even though it was a school night, I'd arranged sleepovers for Jess and George as well. I swear they thought the we-can-do-whatever-we-want train had just pulled in. A lot of things were happening that hadn't before: rooms didn't get tidied, beds weren't made, Brussels sprouts didn't get eaten, and the dining room that never got used was a second playroom. We didn't shout, and we laughed more.

With the kids out for the night, I saw a great opportunity to talk with Pete and share feelings.

We had been able to spend virtually no time alone together. For a while, he had even been sleeping in the spare room, a mutual decision due to the fact that Ollie wanted to sleep with me more and more. At least, that was the excuse I gave at the time. It was partly true.

It's funny. I had already played in my mind how I saw the evening going: trying to get Pete to open up, to talk about Ollie, the kids, us, the future, and another topic we had both avoided: Ollie's funeral.

I saw the evening ahead clearly, or so I thought. I couldn't have been more wrong.

I was really looking forward to the evening. I'd shopped for the special ingredients for our meal: chicken, onion, spices, natural yogurt. I'd also gotten some wine.

I was grateful for the wine. I was nervous, and it relaxed my worried mind. As Pete showered, I poured a second glass, stirring up the sizzling onion and spices, enjoying the hot, pungent aroma.

I wondered how Ollie was doing and made a quick call to learn he was having a whale of a time making brownies. Hearing his faint giggles in the background, I knew I wouldn't have to call again. Now I could relax.

I went to the stereo and selected a CD. Sting crooned "A Thousand Years" while I went back to stirring the pot.

Pete entered the kitchen, freshly showered, his hair still damp, his cheeks rosy from the sting of cologne on newly shaved skin. He looked good. He smelt good, and in one of those quick flashes I was flung back to our early, heady days of new-found love. A smile spread across my face.

"What's up with you?" he asked with a grin.

"Oh, nothing. The wine, I think," I said as I finished my second glass. "It's going down way too well." I told him how Ollie was having a grand ol' time and joked about how his bedtime would likely be a late affair.

He laughed along, adding, "I'm glad he's having a good time."

The way he said that, with a poignancy you

could feel, would have been a perfect intro to the conversation I'd hoped we would have. I had been so frustrated with our not talking about it, yet it was not to be.

I did not venture into the thoughts that plagued us all. "Yes, me too." Not wanting to stay in that conversation, I tasted the curry. "Mmmm, this is going to be so good." And Sting's song soothed on.

For the first time in a very long time, I found myself enjoying the company of this wonderful man, the father of my children. He always did make me laugh, his personality attracting all. If there were a sign above his head, it would say, I'm One of the Good Guys, and anyone would believe it immediately upon meeting him.

We drank, we laughed, and while we enjoyed our Indian fare we remembered.

We remembered *us*.

We celebrated the joys of days past: how we met, family gatherings, the unexpected and merry arrival of Jessica, the joy of welcoming our sons, living on the breadline, how cider had become a good alternative to wine, and sleeping on a sofa bed when I was pregnant with George so Jess could have her own room when we lived in a one-bedroom apartment.

I teased him about getting his first career

break after shoveling sheep shit for so long and how scared he was to use the phone.

He teased me back about how I would never let him forget it, and he was right about that.

"You know it," I joked.

We rewound the eighteen years we had been together, recalling each moment culminating in our move to this great country where we would live the American dream. What a ride it had been. We were fortunate, blessed. Some moments a memory hung in the air, both of us taking it in, not wanting to go *there* and spoil the celebration of what was happening. Maybe, just maybe, we would make it.

The wine flowed as we continued our sharing.

Later, we headed up the stairs, Sting's "After the Rain Has Fallen" drifting melodically behind us. We made love, and it was both beautiful and sad, passion turning to tenderness with all our memories coming together. We held on for a long time, in many ways not wanting it to end, knowing we were saying good-bye to us. After, we lay together in a childlike embrace, curled up in a protective fetal position. Without words, we fell asleep.

Early I awoke and looked at my sleeping husband, grateful for who he was and for giving me my children. I would always love him.

In the sober light of day, I was thankful for

our night of love, our shared memories and celebration of who we were.

In that instant, I knew I could not go back. I could not return to my husband. The good-bye was real. My heart and the voice to which I had not been willing to listen had spoken, and finally I paid attention.

My heart ached for the pain I would cause.

~⁓⚬⚬⁓~

Many good-byes were said in the following weeks.

Ollie wanted to go to Children's "one more time" to play with his friends.

One Friday, though he felt terrible, he told me he had to go to school. I urged him not to, reminding him he could go the following week, but he persisted.

"I have a picture for you, Mummy, a painting I've been working on. I need to finish it."

With some reluctance, I took him in, hoping the extra morphine would be enough.

Two hours later, I picked up my exhausted son.

His teacher, the one to whom he had given his puzzle painting, handed me his completed artwork from the day. "It's a family picture. It's quite beautiful."

Rolled and wrapped in a tube, I tucked it

under my arm and thanked her.

Ollie was too tired to speak. Home by noon, I gave him some more meds and put him to bed. He would sleep through until nine the following day.

Back downstairs, the tube containing his artwork lay on the table. Carefully and slowly, I removed it and smiled at the brightly colored painting before me.

Vaguely I recalled Ollie telling us about a family picture project he had been doing. The teachers had asked the kids to draw or paint a picture that represented their families. While other kids had drawn houses with dogs and matchstick men, Ollie had painted a vase of flowers. Five flowers were in the bright yellow vase, each with a different shaped petal representing each family member. Four of those flowers in full bloom rose majestically with strong stems. The fifth flower had not bloomed; its bud was closed and drooped over the side of the vase.

I did not see then the profound significance of his painting. Perhaps I was not meant to at that moment. Yet I would, and it would happen when I least expected it.

Early spring 2004 brought unusually warm temperatures. The sun was magnificent, shining most days, and our daffodils rose and bunnies hopped in the garden. Ollie relished being outside. Because he was unable to walk now, we would carry him out in his special quilt and sit on the swing with him cocooned in our laps or we would park his black buggy on the deck where he happily watched the bunnies and squirrels playing chase.

Ella perched on her stool in the screen room and made her presence known with a meow here and there. She'd taken to spending more and more time with Ollie as the days went by. I wondered how she'd fare when he left us.

Pete had grudgingly returned to work. His boss had told him he was needed and managed to persuade Pete it would be good for him, "Help take your mind off things."

I disagreed, feeling he would regret time not spent with his son.

At the same time I did not want to press it, fearing it would bring up what was happening with us. Although I had come to a decision, I was not ready to share or discuss it with Pete. Ollie was my only concern.

The irony is that if Pete had not returned to work, then the most profound moment of my life would never have happened.

One afternoon, Ollie and I were lying on the couch.

"Mummy?"

"Yes, baby?"

"I want to go to the train station one last time. I want to surprise Daddy and meet him off the train." His words were barely a whisper, his labored breathing making speech exhausting.

I stroked his head. "Okay, baby."

Then I set about getting the car ready with pillows and blankets.

Ollie told me he wanted to make a card while we waited at the station, so I took along his Thomas the Tank Engine rucksack full of supplies: glitter; stickers, an assortment of colored pens, and his cards.

Parked outside, the radio playing, we waited. I looked at my watch. The train would arrive in about six minutes. *What will I cook for dinner tonight?* I thought.

From the back, Ollie said, "Mummy?" He paused. "How do I write, 'all of you'?"

I spelled it out carefully and slowly.

He carried on.

"Who are you making a card for, Ollie?"

After another pause, he said, "I'm making a card for my family." A moment later, he said, "Because I love you. I love Daddy. I love Jessica. I love Georgie. I love Ella." A pause and then, "And I love the angel inside of me, but I don't know her name, so I'm just going to write, 'I love *all* of you.'"

As he hummed along to the song on the radio, my eyes stung with tears and my skin was prickly. An incredible awareness like no other came over me. Such power and peace enveloped me from the words that had fallen from my child's lips.

Slowly dying before me, *he was not afraid*. As the full impact of his innocent sharing reached into my soul, I gave a silent thank-you to the angel, to God, and to my beautiful child for giving me the gift of peace, of love. I knew when the time came for his final good-bye, I would be able to let him go.

I looked at my watch and heard the faint honk of a train. With two minutes to go, it approached. Taking a deep breath, I gaily said, "Time to go see Daddy, Ollie." I blinked away the threatening tears. "My goodness, he will be so surprised to see you here."

His eyes widened excitedly. "I know! Come on, Mummy. Let's go." Carefully, he put his card

229

back into his rucksack.

I lifted him out of the backseat, and he wrapped his legs around me. I would hold him until the last moment, when the train came to a halt and the doors slid open and he wanted me to put him down so Daddy could see him standing on the platform, waiting for him.

As Pete stepped off the train, another suit, another day, people watched. Pete spotted Ollie waving at him and ran to his child, this child who looked like no other. From the looks, I knew the other passengers sensed *why*.

Daddy scooped him up, and Ollie smiled as people passed, witnesses to something more beautiful than they realized.

Ollie would not visit the station again.

The sunny days continued, and spring break was upon us. Many of our neighbors did not travel or leave for vacations, as they usually did.

At four in the morning one day, I woke suddenly. I looked at my son lying next to me and knew the time was near.

I called Stew. We talked, yet not much, the kindness and sorrow reaching down the line to me as he apologized for not saving my son.

We both wept.

Brushing aside the apology, I thanked him for giving us our Ollie back, a gift of time we narrowly missed.

Hanging up, I lay with my child, selfishly wanting him all to myself.

I told him how much I loved him and how much I would miss his cheeky monkey grin. I told him I thought him incredibly brave and hoped I could be as wonderfully brave as he someday. I told him Daddy, Jess, and Georgie would miss him but would be okay.

He squeezed my hand. He did not speak. I lay with him a little longer.

Then I told him I was going to get Daddy.

I knocked on the spare room door, and Pete came out almost immediately. Seeing the look on my face, he clearly knew what was happening.

Allowing Pete his own time, I went downstairs, lit a cigarette, sat in the screen room, and wept. Ella sat next to me as I stared at the phone. Everything hurt. I picked up the phone and began dialing.

Our home nurse, Maureen, who never took time off work just happened to be free that weekend and wanted to be with us during his final hours.

My friend Toni, who usually worked days, had taken a night shift instead and was able to join us as soon as she left work at five in the morning.

I rang my mum in England. Mum wept, and I consoled her as she told me between sobs how she felt she had failed me as a mother in not being able to protect me from my pain.

After hanging up the phone, I returned to our room, to my husband, and to our son, and we lay together surrounded by his favorite stuffed animals while Thomas the Tank Engine music played in the background. Ticky was tucked safely in his hand as we held our son, and he stayed long enough to say good-bye to all he loved: his beloved brother and sister, friends in the neighborhood, his school friends, his teachers, all of whom took time out of their day to stop by our home and say good-bye to the little boy who had touched their lives so deeply.

A sense of beauty, of grace, filled the room. I could feel it on my skin. Through tear-blurred vision, I saw the mounds of tissues on the floor resembling clouds. The air was light.

The day now evening, good-byes said, we were alone with our child.

Pete and I lay with our precious son, arms wrapped around him, around each other. With Ollie's last breath approaching, Thomas stopped playing . . .

CHAPTER 15
All Aboard!

In the blackness of grief, I went back to my twenties and waited on the platform for the train to arrive to take me to London Bridge station. I wasn't going to work. I was going to kill myself.

The weird thing about suicide is you don't actually think about it. You don't wake up one morning and say, "Today's the day I end my life." At least I didn't. I just wanted to sleep. My whole body was so damn tired. I had no other focus. Sleep was good; sleep was warm; it caressed you and took care of you when no one else did. The seduction of its nothingness was overwhelmingly powerful.

The confusion of my orientation as well as the trauma inflicted on me as a child had finally caught up. Although I was dressed for work, two things were different.

I wore slippers, and I knew I wouldn't be boarding.

The station was busy with commuters, a sea of black and grey suits holding coffee cups, reading newspapers, staring into space. The usual. Each lost in thought, no one batted an eyelid at my slippers.

I stood at the edge looking down, feeling floaty. I heard the train and looked up. It was barely visible in the distance. I swayed back and forth, mesmerized by the clickety-clack, clickety-clack. Getting louder. Drawing near. A rumbling shook the platform, and a wind picked up. Engine power. The pungent aroma of fuel filled my nostrils.

I couldn't see or hear the commuters. I only saw the train and a light, blinding and eerily warm. Despite the hurt in my eyes, they were locked to the light.

I had no time to go to sleep because I was hit by an overwhelming clarity. *No, this is not your way.* As the light and train whooshed past, I was flung into the arms of a man wearing a trilby, the kind of hat Frank Sinatra and the Rat Pack used to wear in the good ol' Vegas days.

"You okay?" he said, then added, "You're wearing slippers."

"I know."

I don't recall leaving the station. I don't recall thinking about anything. My life simply continued.

Thanks to a train.

Fighting with the darkness, I wondered if it was evil's cruel joke. *Well, sorry, me lovely, but I just had to save the best for last.*

Images tortured my mind: the pronouncement of death, 6:57 p.m. Clinging to my dead child. Seeing him leave our home in a black plastic sack. Returning to an empty bed, an empty heart, an empty life.

The crashing noise of pain in my head was not eased by the alcohol or pills. *I should have gone then. I should have gone then. Oh God, why?* I desperately yearned for nothingness. *Anything but this.*

I'd failed to anticipate the power of grief.

In the wreckage, I also failed to notice my family.

I was invisible, lost in a black hole. I was not strong. I did not hold my head high and put on a brave face. I was not one of those mothers who went to church and shared with the community, "Thanks to God, we'll come through this." I was the mother who would slap you in the face if you dared to say, "Well, at least he's safe in the arms of Jesus," as you handed me an apple pie.

I felt abandoned, forgotten, unworthy, unloved. A failure.

I was nothing.

I observed Pete through a fog, drowning in his sorrow, drenched in wine and antidepressants.

I watched my children grieve in their own ways

yet could not go to them. I had cruel thoughts of grief, jealousy that they were here when Ollie was not. I never wished them any malice or harm; I just couldn't understand their *normalness*. When they'd laugh or want to go to the movies, I'd get astonishingly *angry*. A simple act or moment would leave me deeply wounded that they could do these things and Ollie could not. Ashamed, I did not share these horrible thoughts.

Pete and I had moments of ugliness I never thought possible from two people who had once loved each other so deeply. He wanted to make love, and I recoiled as if touched by some grotesque monster.

He would vent his fury. "Ollie's dead, but I'm not and I want to fuck!"

And the demon in me would rise up and slash his heart. "Well, go fuck someone else because I don't give a bloody shit!"

The truth of the matter was that I was desperate to be held, desperate to *feel*, yet I couldn't stand to be hugged, let alone anything else. The pain of unworthiness was consuming.

In those wretched moments, my failure as a mother was fuelled to limits of which I couldn't believe I was capable, so I retreated to the safety of darkness where I belonged.

I could not reach out to anyone. How could I when I could not reach myself?

However, someone would reach out to me.

One night, I was drifting further and further into my hellhole when a voice spoke inside my head. At first I thought it was the alcohol playing tricks, so I ignored it.

It continued.

Suddenly, I recognized the voice singing, "Oh, yes, it's great to be an engine as you speed along. . . . Puff puff puffing along all day." It was a happy, upbeat song, one I knew only too well. Where the hell was it coming from?

"I love you, Mummy, always and forever."

"Ollie?" I whispered.

He smiled his big cheeky grin and continued singing, "Thomas the Tank Engine. Toot, toot!"

I laughed out loud at the insanity of the situation. "This can't be happening. I'm going mad. I'm actually going bloody mad," I shouted to the darkness. I looked at the bedroom door, waiting for Pete or the kids to tell me to keep quiet, but no one came.

"There's Gordon and Henry, Edward, James and Toby, Annie and Clarabel, and don't forget Percy." Ollie giggled.

What the—? This is stupid. I tried to rationalize what was happening. *This is just utterly ridiculous.*

"I love you, Mummy, always and forever." I saw him smile his perfect smile. "And you have to tell them."

"What?" I said out loud.

"I love you, Mummy, and you have to tell them."

"Tell them what?"

A pause. "You know."

And Ollie returned to singing his favorite of the Thomas songs, the same one that had played as he lay dying in our arms. "Oh, yes, it's great to be an engine as you speed along. . . . Puff puff puffing along all day."

I relished his beautiful presence.

I was a wreck. My pain was enormous, yet somehow I summoned everything I had to get out of bed. My body was slow, awkward, heavy. My eyes were swollen and sore, yet still the tidal wave of tears flowed without mercy as my sobs racked in unison.

I headed downstairs and found myself sitting at the computer. With curser flashing, I stared at the blank screen momentarily and out of nowhere, two words popped into my head and I typed them. *All Aboard.*

I had begun.

What I was beginning, I didn't really know. It didn't matter. I somehow sensed it was right, good, and important.

While Pete and I argued about our son's funeral, I wrote. I wrote *everything*, and the words came fast and furious.

Pete wanted to bury our son, put him in a coffin, and lower him into the earth, in what I saw as a depressing church ceremony. The thought horrified me. I could not imagine, seeing it as somehow inappropriate. What I came to understand was that Pete just wanted it to be done and to move on.

I wanted to celebrate our son on a day that was truly about him and not some sermon delivered by someone who didn't even know our child. I wanted a memorial that represented everything about Ollie. I wanted kids to just be kids and play, be entertained by silly clowns and magicians, giggle, play dress-up with friends, and of course enjoy his beloved train sets. Just a regular day with family and friends who would also gather to share their thoughts. This was how I saw our son's funeral.

After some persuading, Pete finally gave in and we agreed on two things. First, that we would have Ollie cremated, his ashes to be spread at a time and place yet to be determined. Second, that we would hold a day of celebration in his honor.

We chose a day perfectly fitting, the day our son was born, June 19. With the date two and a half months away, the family in England had time to make arrangements and I had time to plan. I booked a clown who did magic tricks and a professional videographer to record the events.

Leading up to the day, people asked, "But what if it rains, Deb?"

I smiled and said quite truthfully, "It's not going to.

It's going to be a beautiful day. Just you wait and see."

And it was.

The sky was a blazing blue and the sun shone down, smiling with us.

The celebration took place in our back garden at the end of a private cul-de-sac, perfect for the YMCA's climbing wall and the local fire truck that delighted the goggle-eyed kids from the neighborhood.

Under lawn tents were Ollie's desk, schoolwork, toys, special quilt, buggy, and a memory notebook where people could leave their personal thoughts of him. The kids played with the playhouse, the dress-up box, Ollie's train sets, and his tricycle that went tring-tring.

Childlike songs and classical music floated across the neighborhood. Our family, friends, neighbors, and even our dear friend, the Pied Piper of Children's Memorial, Dr. Stew Goldman, thronged in. Laughter, tears, lots of hugs, and a sense of peace and pure joy filled the place. Huge black-and-white photographs of Ollie were draped down the back of our house, courtesy of our friend Andrew Taylor who had taken those pictures the previous Halloween. Amongst the photos were splashed words describing Ollie: *playful, brave, cute, inspiring, courageous, funny.* A microphone was on the deck, where people could share memories of our child, this brave little boy who loved trains and inspired so many.

I continued to write and began sharing my writing with family and friends, sending off segments as I finished them. I also sent them to the nurses at Children's and to Stew. I don't know why I made that decision. It just happened.

I went back to the beginning and relived the past two years. Standing on the outside looking in, I saw things differently, saw it all.

Some days, I could barely write a sentence as grief gripped me. On others, I wrote several pages. It was a cathartic process, like having my own private therapist without the fee.

It was raw, brutal in its honesty, and shocking in places. Grief at its finest. I didn't care what people thought. I just had to get it out. There was a sense of urgency. Importance.

I learned much about myself as I wrote. I would laugh at my own writing, then feel terribly alone as tears fell onto the keyboard.

I didn't always eat. I smoked. I drank coffee. I drank wine. I rarely showered. Mostly, I just grieved and shared it with Mr. Word Document, then pressed the send button and off it went into the Universe, which is when the magic truly began.

I started to receive e-mails in response to what I

was sharing. People were moved, inspired. They asked, "Can I share this with someone, Deb? I think it could really help them." The nurses called to tell me my writing spurred them on through the rough days.

I was both moved and elated, aware that my son's spirit was making an impact and would not be lost in the ever-rising statistics after all.

It was like a domino effect. As I shared, others did too. I had a deep sense of paying it forward. Incredibly, I received e-mails from people I didn't even know from as far afield as California, Germany, Key West, and Australia. To this day, I still do.

The messages were different yet the same: "I was so moved by Ollie and his story. Thank you for letting me into your world. God bless you."

One e-mail truly moved me:

"I felt compelled to write you and share just how touched I was by your story, which was passed on to me by a friend. I have three sons, all of whom have been in trouble with the law over the years, two right now who are in jail. There have been many times I have wanted to give up on my sons when, in moments of helplessness, I would allow despair to drag me down and angrily turn away from my sons because I felt ashamed of them.

"Reading your story, Ollie's story, affected me deeply. One minute I was crying, the next laughing, yet out of it all I came away wanting to go to my boys and simply tell them I loved them. I will never give up on my boys, and I wanted to thank you for this lovely gift of a book and know that I will be passing it along to those who, like me, kind of got lost and need to find their way.

"I'm so happy I got to know your Ollie. He will always be in my heart. God bless you, Debi."

Many mothers said after reading my story, they yelled less at their kids and hugged them more.

These messages were not only telling me that something special was happening; they told me I was healing as a mother, and I was so utterly grateful for that.

One day I received a call from Stew, who asked if he could read part of my segments in an address to residents entering pediatric oncology. He thought what I had written regarding the initial diagnosis would benefit them greatly.

"They need to hear it from a family, Deb," he explained. "They need to know the emotional impact from a parent's perspective as well as the medical, and your honesty is powerful and real."

Both honored and flabbergasted, I humbly agreed. It was a wonderful feeling of pride to know my son's passing would impact these young people entering the world so close to Ollie's heart, and I sensed something more was happening. I sensed purpose behind the madness and felt it was important I continue.

As I wrote, profound changes began in me. In truth, they had begun the moment of our son's diagnosis. I was transformed, as we all were. What I did not know at that point was where the changes would lead.

Through the murky waters of grief, I had begun to see reason. As I continued to write and share my deepest thoughts, the waters began to clear, allowing me to see more as each day passed.

Among the e-mails, one came from Kristin Leigh Hughes, senior gift director at Children's Memorial. She shared gracious words about my story and then told me about an event Children's hosts each year to raise funds for the hospital. It was Eric & Kathy's 36 Hour Radiothon. The famous hosts set up the station in the lobby of Children's and invited families to share their experiences, some of which were truly harrowing yet equally inspiring. "Would you like to participate?" she wrote.

It was only a few weeks away and only five months after Ollie's passing. Part of me wanted to. Part of me was terrified I wouldn't be able to keep it together. I told Pete and the kids about it, but no one wanted to go. The grief was too raw, which I understood.

I decided to go anyway. When I pulled into the car park and saw the familiar building, my hands suddenly got clammy and my heart raced. Walking into the lobby, I shook, my emotions ready to burst. I took deep breaths while I checked into reception.

Meeting Kristin, I shared a tearful hug.

"How are you, love?" she said. "You okay to do this?"

I nodded, gulping down the threatening chokes.

Eric and Kathy were introducing a family, and their song began to play. Rows of volunteers manning the phones sat behind them, dabbing their eyes as the story of a child filled the airwaves, an all too familiar tale.

I was supposed to follow the family, but being in our home away from home without my Ollie was wretchedly overwhelming. Without warning, grief gripped me and I had to get out fast.

I managed to make it to my car.

Safe inside, I exploded in pain, annoyed I could not control it.

Human nature, when thrown into the unpredictable world of grief was a minefield. It didn't matter how lightly I tiptoed around that field or if I thought I had X-ray vision and could see what was coming. I could not. I was utterly at the mercy of human nature. One minute I might've been walking through beautiful daisies with the sun shining warmly on my face. I'd be quite happy during the Christmas season to wish those nice Good Samaritan folks happy holidays as they rang their bells merrily; then suddenly out of nowhere it would be dark and heavy and I'd feel pain in every pore of my skin. Even my eyes would hurt. And what the hell happened to the daisies? Where was the sun? It would have been blown to smither-eens. Then would come the I-don't-give-a-shit attitude when darkness drug me under, kicking and screaming, and the kids would go without their favorite cookies because I'd fear going to the store, telling those nice Good Samaritan folks to fuck Christmas, and hitting them over the head with their stupid annoying bells.

This was the reality of grief.

Yet I'd made a start. I had at least entered the hospital.

The following year, I returned to share my story, which I have done each year since.

It's strange how much I miss Children's. You may imagine that a parent would be glad to leave such a place, yet the bonds forged in this wonderful hospital we came to know as home are strong. Like the kids who reside there.

I miss seeing Stew.

I even miss staying over the weekend for Ollie's therapy and ordering up breakfast after sleeping hap-hazardly in a chair and then complaining about it.

I miss the nurses and their jovial bantering with Ollie.

I miss the smiles and hellos from the girls who worked the front reception desk and were always ask-ing me for fit tips and saying, "Where *do* you get your hair done, honey?"

I miss the guy in the tiny coffee shop who didn't know my name but always knew how I liked my cup of joe.

I miss the kind lady in the gift shop with the funny hairdo who always made sure there were magic pads in stock because she knew how much Ollie loved them and that he would want not one, not two, but three. Always three.

I miss the organized chaos of the oncology day clinic. I miss watching the kids take rides on their IV poles and playing Candy Land in the playroom. I miss the staff and wish I could give them hugs for all the times I was a bitch to them, which means we'd be pretty much smooching all day.

I miss the canteen staff who loved to joke about my accent and doted on the cute little English boy who always ordered a piece of chocolate fudge cake, his favorite. Their eyes filled with tears when I told them he was gone.

I miss the guy in the parking lot who hands out tickets all day with a smile and a joke about the Sox or Cubs.

I even miss complaining about the valet parking and the fact that they could never understand a damn word I said.

I miss Maureen, our home nurse, and her brilliant sense of humor. Only she could make me laugh about the color of puke and crap or the funny side of memory loss: "Yeah, I can read the same story to him every night and he thinks it's a new one."

I miss everything.

I miss Ollie.

I think about kids like Ollie who are still battling constantly. At certain times of the day, my mind wanders to what they are doing. At eight the breakfast trolley is coming around along with coffee for the parents; at three sharp they're playing hospital bingo. Kids struggling with infections are frozen in fear when the little man with wiry hair comes to draw blood; their pic lines, surgically inserted, are already in use and a line is needed to draw blood, but he will be quick and the pain will be brief.

This flow of fighting for life is continuous, steady. My thoughts of these brave children are permanent. I can't get them out of my head. This is part of my path, wherever it may lead. I am not meant to remain forever lost in grief.

Somewhere within the trauma was the purpose. Staying connected with Children's along with the staff and families was much a part of it. What the future held for me I did not know, yet I did know with utter faith that I was on track and headed in the right direction.

I continued to write, continued to connect with people. In the process, I pondered my life, my future. People who shared their inspirations allowed me to come out of the darkness and into something new, albeit unknown. These glorious moments would come quite unexpectedly, whether standing in line at the grocery store or from my platform as a teacher during class.

I recall Kathy, who works the checkout at our local grocery store. She always had a kind word for Ollie and had known him all his life. Scanning products, she looked up at me. "I'm glad you came in today, Deb. I want you to know that Ollie has been on my mind a lot lately. He gives me great strength. That little boy was the bravest human being I ever met." She was teary eyed.

I thanked her, sharing a hug.

I would later find out that Kathy had been diagnosed with breast cancer. Kathy is now a cancer survivor and often shares with folks how a little boy called Ollie inspired her.

Another time, on the first anniversary of Ollie's passing, I was scheduled to teach class and I almost didn't make it as grief took hold. Spurred on by my son's brave spirit, I went. During the cool-down period of class, I shared with my members that I was grateful to them for lifting my spirits on a day that was very difficult for me. I played the song, "Peace and Love" and fought hard to keep my tears at bay, as did many of the members.

Several came up to me afterward and shared hugs. One took my hands in hers and squeezed them tightly, saying, "I just want to touch you, because *you* touch *me* every day. Thank you, and God bless you."

Deeply moved, I was humbly grateful, aware of this beautiful *happening* that was taking place and lighting my world. These precious inspirations would continue and to this day still do.

Pete and I were living together but not as a couple, and both of us calmly accepted it. It was as if we knew we were coming to the end of us but did not want to address it yet.

He returned to work after a short period, accompanied by his antidepressants. Meanwhile I stayed home, my fingertips bashing at the keyboard.

Jess and George got back into the swing of school and usual activities, interrupted here and there with days when our need to share Ollie arose. On those days, we would watch movies, play the games they liked, draw pictures, do little but talk, or say nothing at all. Some days the kids wanted to be left alone in their rooms, and I would let them.

Just days after Ollie passed, George drew a picture of himself on a big green hill. Ollie was in a painted blue sky, wearing a big smile and angel wings above a brightly painted rainbow. Written across it were the words *Brothers Forever*.

George, my first special boy, was incredibly close to Ollie. One day, when the grief was still new, it came crashing down on him. I wrote about it in my journal that day:

George is angry. He hates school. I know he doesn't hate school. He hates that Ollie is gone and is taking it out on school, the one thing that Ollie loved the most.

For the last two nights he has slept in my bed and woken tearful. Last week he asked if he could stay home, have one of our Ollie days where we watch a home movie, eat food Ollie liked best, look at photographs, and share our memories of him. I called the school and said he didn't feel well, which was true, for his heart is broken.

As adults we can take time from our jobs, be officially declared bereaved, and take a leave of absence. With our children we automatically assume that school is the best place for them and don't consider that they too need time themselves to openly grieve. In the comfort and safety of home we can cry, scream, and wail without fear of others observing. We can share our fears and loss and curl up on the floor clutching a photo of our loved one.

In school, George's mind is taken away from his grief, which is not a bad thing, but it was clear to me that he needed to do his own screaming, which school could not afford him.

We talked of how much it hurt not to hug Ollie

or be able to hear him. How much we missed seeing him and how hurtful it was to see his train sets and toys down in the basement gathering dust along with his school bag and his little gold chest of stickers he so adored.

We went down and tearfully brought out one of his train sets. Amidst the playing, I held my ten-year-old son and rocked him as I had when he'd been a baby. He wailed and sobbed, moaning just one word over and over and over: "Ollie. Ollie. Ollie. Ollieeee."

"Shhhhh, baby. I know, baby. I know." I stroked my lovely boy's hair, hating this grief of his, the pain and yearning for his brother so.

I held him until his sobs grew silent. Handing him a tissue, I told him I wanted to show him something and led him to my fitness studio. "You know," I said, "when I feel really angry, sweetie, this is where I come, and this is what I do." Putting on my boxing gloves, standing astride my seventy-five-pound bag, I landed punches. Hard. "It's a horrible feeling when we feel so angry not to be able to show it, but I have to. I have to let it out, and you know what? I feel ten times better after. Wanna try?" I pulled off my gloves and handed them to him.

He smiled. "Okay," he said with a sniff.

He started tentatively, almost softly, but that didn't last. Pretty soon he was landing them hard and fast as his breathing quickened. Getting sweaty, he landed punch after punch.

"Wow!" I yelled. "You really know how to punch, little man. You go, George!"

Then, quite suddenly, he stopped and started laughing. "I feel silly." He giggled.

"Who cares?" I laughed with him and landed one or two with my bare hands. "It feels good, doesn't it?"

"Yeah, but I still feel silly." Breathless, he took off the gloves and said with a chuckle, "Do you remember that time when we were sitting at the table having tea and you had put sliced bananas on Ollie's plate?"

I nodded with a smile. I knew where this was going.

He went on, still laughing. "And he didn't want them but wanted you to think he had eaten them?"

"Yeah, I remember."

George really began to laugh. "He was so funny. He took all those slices of banana and tucked them under his plate, all around, so you wouldn't see."

"Well, it was pretty clever," I said, laughing with him at the memory. I had taken the plate away and found a perfect circle of bananas on his placemat. Giggling at his plan, I didn't have the heart to make him eat them, so I pretended I hadn't noticed.

"I bet you didn't know about the vitamins." George laughed.

"What about the vitamins?" I didn't know what the heck he was talking about.

Even with all the meds Ollie had to take daily, as strange as it may seem, I always thought it really important that he take a multivitamin. Even though they were teddy shaped and strawberry flavored, he grimaced. Nonetheless he took them, or so I thought.

Georgie, still giggling, led me by the hand back upstairs to Ollie's bathroom. "Look, this is what Ollie used to do. I haven't moved this one."

At first, I couldn't see what he was trying to show me. Then, upon closer inspection, I saw. Tucked neatly, almost fitting the shape perfectly, inside the hinge of the door, the chosen hiding place, was a little pink teddy vitamin practically waving at me.

"Oh, that cheeky monkey," I exclaimed. "Well, he really got me on that one, didn't he?" I laughed, and I swear Ollie was probably laughing too. We decided to leave his teddy vitamin where it was. Every time I peed in that bathroom, I smiled when I looked at the door.

George needed that day. If he needs another, I will let him have it. We talked more and shared our thoughts of Ollie's courage. No matter that we could no longer see or hear him, he would be with us always.

"He's a part of you, Georgie. Forever. I had you in my tummy, and then Ollie was in the same place. You have the same blood, the same eyes, the same skin. He's inside of you now. You know how you can sense him sometimes?"

He nodded. "Sometimes, I feel him on the bus."

"Well, that doesn't surprise me. He loved to ride the bus with you, George. And I know what you mean, like the way I sense him sometimes when I'm about to switch off the TV, and his voice in my head yells, 'Hey, I was watching that!'"

We joked more about when we felt Ollie with us, and George said, "I still wish Ollie hadn't gone, Mummy."

"I know, sweetie. I didn't want him to go either." I paused. "But he had to, and he was incredibly brave. Even though he loves us all very much, he knew he would leave this world and he wasn't scared. He knew there was a reason. He knew it was really, really important. Ollie always knew that, and he wants us to know now more than ever he's happy in his heaven. He's like he was before he got sick, and in that summer he was tumor free. He comes to you to tell you that. To let you know."

George continued listening, and I hoped it all made some kind of sense to him. How much does a ten-year-old understand of such a loss?

"I mean, when you sense him," I said, "it's a good feeling, right? A happy feeling?"

He nodded.

"Well, that's because he is happy. He always was, even when he was sick, and he wants to keep that in your heart, little man. Ollie loves all of us and lots of other people, and I think right now Ollie is helping a child just like him. He comes to us, but I know he goes to others. He knows that's what he needs to do, what he wants to do: to help another child not feel so scared and help them to be brave, just the way he was."

George smiled and nodded, and I felt he did understand what I was telling him.

Grief and love. Two powerful emotions, yet only one can heal.

Not long after Ollie passed, twelve-year-old Jessica was assigned to write about a favorite memory. This is what she wrote:

In Memory of My Little Brother

Cancer. The word my family dreaded for two years. My brother was an incredibly creative person. He loved art, the color red, and his favorite TV show, *Thomas the Tank Engine*, but his most favorite thing to do was be with his family. Unfortunately, Ollie couldn't do that anymore. Sadly, my brother passed away on March 26, 2004, from a disease called cancer.

It all started when little five-year-old Ollie Tibbles started being sick and having a lot of headaches. We went to our family doctor to see if everything was okay. He said everything was fine, but the headaches and sickness got worse. We took Ollie to a pediatrician sometime a while later. We got some MRIs (Medical Resonance Images) done, and there was bad news.

Ollie had a brain tumor, which also spread to his spine. He had to have brain surgery immediately. He couldn't function properly after the surgery and was in the hospital for weeks, maybe months. We visited him a couple of times. I can still remember the clean smell that hospital had.

After Ollie had his surgery, the doctors at the hospital told us that Ollie had cancer. Ollie then had to have radiation therapy and chemotherapy to try and kill all the cancer in his body. He had to have radiation and chemotherapy every week for sixty-eight weeks, which was hard on my mum, who was the one who had to drive him to the hospital every day and back home again. (The hospitals were Children's Memorial and Northwestern, all the way in downtown Chicago.) It was always my mum because my dad worked in another state and didn't come home until Friday night every other week then would have to leave again on a Sunday.

My brother was terribly sick with all the therapy he had to go through, with all the side effects and stuff, so really he couldn't be a normal five-year-old little boy. But he was still a humorous, cute little boy that everybody fell in love with whenever they met him. I remember my mum telling me that the nurses would always sign up to be with Ollie whenever he was coming in to the hospital. He was such a fun little boy to be around. He always lightened up the moment even if he was in terrible pain and was sick.

After battling for two years—twenty-four hours a day, seven days a week—Ollie eventually died at age seven. It was March 26, 2004, at 6:57 p.m. My brother died in the arms of my mum and dad, surrounded by his little stuffed animals, toys, and Ticky, with the sound of music he used to love.

In conclusion, this memory isn't my favorite memory because obviously it's sad and just not happy. Yet my brother was a great little boy, and that's the memory I'm talking about. My favorite memory was my little brother.

I saw changes in my children. They argued less, cared more, and somehow seemed older.

Meanwhile, Pete and I tried to stay calm and accepting of our relationship as we fought our own wars, wanting to hold it together for the kids, then realizing we could not.

Sadly, it is common that when a family loses a child, the parents divorce, the pain too much. It would be easy for me to say that is what happened to us, and in some respect, it is true. However, facing the *real* truth is much harder and takes guts.

The courage my child displayed awoke me to my own truth and courage. As I struggled with my identity and what I wanted in my life, I recalled a conversation I'd had with Ollie during a quiet snuggle time.

Lying on the couch, his head resting on my lap, he said, "It will be okay, Mummy. It doesn't matter what color you are." He stroked Ticky on my hand. "You should not be afraid. You are like a rainbow, Mummy, and everyone loves rainbows."

I did not respond right away. Sensing his wise old soul, I took in his words, understood immediately what they meant, and was struck with love and awe. "I love you, baby." What I meant was, "Thank you, baby."

How could I ignore such innocent prophecy? How could I ignore myself? I felt doing so would be an insult to Ollie and also to me.

⚜

I did not return to teaching, choosing instead to write in my journal. I continued to share it, and it reached the hands of Debbie Purcell, a major events coordinator at the Make-A-Wish Foundation. She, in turn, asked my permission to share it with others. As always, I agreed.

I wrote for almost a year, finishing in March of 2005. Then I put the writing to bed, feeling in many ways cleansed and new, stripped of some of the pain. It was a good feeling.

People asked if I planned to publish the work. They encouraged it, yet I somehow sensed it was not meant to be published. At least, not yet. For some reason I felt it wasn't the right time, so I did not pursue it.

A few weeks later, I got a phone call from Debbie Purcell. "I just finished reading your book, and it's amazing, Deb," she said. "I'd love to talk about it some more and meet with you for coffee if that's possible."

I thanked her and told her I was really looking forward to meeting and sharing Ollie's story.

We met and talked for over two hours, sharing Ollie's wish and the impact it had made on the foundation and its patrons. She said it meant more to her now that she knew the full story of my son's courage and how his strength and inspiration had given many people so much hope. Teary eyed, she said that seeing the journey we had taken had made a profound impact on her.

I felt humbled and grateful for her kind thoughts. As she shared these thoughts of this quiet awareness of something truly special happening, I was aware once again that I was on the right track.

I didn't know where it led. The voice deep within didn't tell me, and it didn't matter. I would stay on this track regardless and be led blindly to wherever I was supposed to go.

A few weeks later, Deb called again to tell me about an annual event the Make-A-Wish Foundation hosts, the biggest of the year: the Make-A-Wish Grand Ball, a huge gala on the Chicago charity scene. "And the foundation would like you to be the guest speaker, Debi."

"What?" I said, dumbfounded, then quickly added, "Thank you. My gosh. Wow! I don't know what to say."

"Well, I hope you will say yes."

And then panic set in. "But I've never spoken in my life, Deb. Are you kidding me? I mean, really? Me?" The thought terrified me. What the hell would I say?

"Oh, Debi, I just know you'd be great. You have a wonderful way with words, and Ollie's story is incredibly touching. I just know your presence would truly benefit the foundation. Please at least think about it," she said hopefully.

In both shock and joy I said I would think about it, and we hung up.

To be asked was, of course, an honor. I held on to that while I battled my fears of not being good enough, of cracking under the pressure, of losing it in front of everyone. I decided to accept anyway.

When I called Deb with the news, I could sense her smiling at my decision. She explained how the event was planned. My speech would be the one guests would want to see. The timing of it was important for the other speakers. There would be representatives of the foundation, volunteers, and wish children. I was to send photos and video footage to be used, and a rehearsal would take place prior to the event.

Just talking about the plans fueled my nerves. I wanted to back out.

Debbie picked up on my anxiety and reassured me repeatedly.

Something happened later that finally allowed me

to accept the honor.

The phone rang.

"Debi," Deb said, something about her voice sounding odd, "there is something you are not going to believe." A pause.

"What?" I said. "What? Deb, what?" The hair on the back of my neck suddenly stood up.

"Well, a couple of things really. I just got news of the location of the event." Another long pause.

"Yeah, and?" I prompted, unable to stand it.

"It's being held at Union Station, the place where Ollie had his wish," she said excitedly.

"Oh my God," I screamed. I could hardly believe it. "No way!" My tummy did a flip. I smiled and said something about Ollie having some kind of role in this, and we both laughed.

She continued, "Yes, well, there's more, Deb. I've also had the designers send me the plate of the invitation we plan to use, and I'm sending you one in the mail." Her voice was practically shaky at this point. "I couldn't believe my eyes when I saw it, Deb. After all, they don't know it's you speaking for us. I'm looking at it right now, and right across the front in big black letters are the words *All Aboard* and then right underneath, *For the Make-A-Wish Grand Ball*."

Her words hung in the air, and I felt my skin tingle and a wave of something flowing through me. "Oh my God!" I kept repeating.

"I know, I know."

I shared the news of my speaking engagement with family and friends, and everyone offered support and congratulations. The opportunity was a much-needed boost for Pete and the kids as well. We were all terribly excited. Pete cast aside money worries, splurging on new togs for the black-tie event and reserving a limo to take us and friends there.

My journey was leading to Union Station and the podium and a moment so profound it would mark the beginning of my true calling and future destiny.

CHAPTER 16
Make-A-Wish Grand Ball

During the early stages of Ollie's therapy, we'd been invited to a wedding in the neighborhood, and I'd excitedly told the kids that the couple were planning a trip to the Bahamas for their honeymoon.

Ollie looked at me and said, "What's a honeymoon? That's a funny word. What is it, Mummy?"

I tried to explain what it meant—love, happiness, playfulness, forgetting your troubles, and basically having *the* most glorious time. "Apart from having you, of course," I added, giving him a hug.

He giggled. "Oooooh, I get it."

Truth be told, I really wasn't sure he did.

Now only a few weeks away from the ball when I would share Ollie's life from a stage, I had a dream. You know when you have a dream sometimes and you *know* it's a dream? When it's really good and you're aware you're about to wake up and you try to force yourself back into it? Or on the other end of the scale, it's nightmarish and you just want out of it, even to the point you find yourself saying so to try and get yourself out of the dream?

This was different. This felt real. The thought of staying in or getting out of the dream never arose. I was just *there*.

I was standing on nothing, and everyone was with me—family, friends, and a whole sea of faces I didn't know but did, and we were staring up at a stage. For some reason it felt as though we were in a school play, and I could see the principal and aides from Ollie's school in the crowd waving happily at me. I waved back and continued to look at the stage expectantly. I was waiting for something but didn't quite know what it was. I was nervous and excited. I looked around for Pete but couldn't see him, yet this did not worry me. Somehow I knew he was in the crowd. Jess and George were next to me looking up at the stage, both smiling and gaily chatting together. Although I heard no distinct words from anyone's lips, there was an audible babble that was pleasant and warm on the ear.

Suddenly the invisible stage was full of children, so many more than there had been just seconds before, and the audience below was all around, their arms outstretched. As I gazed up at the children who seemed to be ages four through eight, they began to dive from the stage, elegantly and with supreme grace, into the arms below them, giggling and laughing as they did so. The adults, whom I just assumed to be parents, caught them with ease.

Suddenly I was filled with extreme panic. I yelled out to no one in particular, "Ollie can't do that," but my shouts fell on deaf ears. I mouthed the words, *Someone has to carry him. He can't walk. He's sick. Where's his buggy?* because my voice was silent and I was terrified.

Suddenly I was alone, and I looked up to see Ollie smiling and waving at me with his cheeky monkey grin.

Although I was alone, I found I was calm. Ollie looked like he had before disease had ravaged his body. He was not bald. He was not skeletal. He had no burn marks and was not bloated. He was simply *perfect*.

Slowly, gracefully, he dived. Like a magnificent eagle, he swooped down in wonderful silence, and I was immediately aware of a warm, comforting light accompanied by a beautiful, indescribable humming.

With glorious ease he came to my outstretched arms, and we basked in the love that was felt so intensely. The moment seemed to go on forever, and my skin tingled. The happiness I cannot describe, only that what I felt was so utterly *real* to me.

Ollie cupped my face in his hands and said something to me which at first I could not comprehend. He did not say, "I love you." It was almost as though those words were not needed, for I knew their message already and could feel it wrapped all around me. As I began to wake, he repeated the words softly and lovingly. They were the *only* words he said: "I am giving you back your honeymoon, Mummy."

The ball was drawing near, and Jess and I fretted about what to wear. We went shopping for gowns and had a lovely time trying on clothes, hats, shoes, and fancy shawls. It was so fun to be with her, walking around the endless stores and complaining about our aching feet the way women do. Seeing our smiles and hearing our laughter, no one would know what we had been through, and I was grateful. It was a joy.

Finally, the evening was upon us. In the limo, we sipped champagne and toasted the special evening. With a shaky hand, I applied more lipstick.

We arrived at the Great Hall of Chicago Union Station to a buzz of anticipation and were led to our table at the front of the huge stage. Elegant drapes hung majestically from the ceiling, and two enormous video screens displayed the familiar Make-A-Wish logo. Pictures of smiling children and their families, of wishes past and present, beamed at us.

The hall was alive with people from all walks of life: previous wish children now grown, wish granters, volunteers, families of wish children, philanthropists, bankers, celebrities, secretaries, businesspeople, doctors, nurses, and those attending for the first time courtesy of friends.

My heart was thumping madly, my nerves now rising. I gazed at the steps leading up to the stage and suddenly wished I wasn't wearing the ridiculously high heels I had so carefully chosen a few days earlier.

I looked at my watch. Two hours before I was on. The wait was excruciating.

I barely touched my meal but drank two glasses of wine. I pondered a third but quickly reconsidered. *I don't want to fall up those bloody stairs*, I thought. I was sweating now and kept dabbing my cheeks with powder to combat the annoying shine.

Prior to my slot, dignitaries from the foundation had spoken, explaining its mission and sharing other stories. With over nine hundred people present, I had noticed with increasing concern that the room was noisy, the buzz of conversation seemingly getting louder. Even with the microphone, speakers were not always heard. Worse, sometimes people were not paying attention.

My nerves were further fueled when I learned that television crews were filming the event.

That's all I bloody need, my brain screamed. *Beamed across Chicagoland for all to see—a shaking Debi in all her sweaty, shiny glory.*

When it was time, I wanted to be sick and go to the loo all at once.

I waited for my introduction, worrying that no one would want to listen to me.

What happened next is kind of a dream.

I looked down at my speech with blurred vision. In my head, I wished Ollie were with me. *I need you, baby. Make me proud, my son.*

I heard my name followed by a ripple of applause that I barely noticed. The music we'd selected played as I walked up to the stage to accompany the video footage of our son. There were pictures of him. His beautiful face in a snapshot taken what seemed like a hundred years ago, the day his wish was fulfilled to be a train driver, on board his most favorite of trains, the Metra passenger train, which reminded him of London's double-decker buses.

I fought back tears as the memories flooded back, the pain of missing him immediately present. I stood shaking and trying to breathe while I waited for what seemed like an eternity for the video and music to stop so I could begin.

It stopped. Audience chatter buzzed. I stood in front of the microphone and looked out at the sea of faces, so many that I could not make all of them out. They seemed to disappear in the distance of the Great Hall.

For years I had donned a microphone while teaching my classes. I had cued, joked, shared about my family, my thoughts, my life. Yet in that moment it felt like the first time, and I was scared of my own voice.

Somebody took a picture, and the flash made me jump.

To this day I do not recall what I said exactly. I know that I started out following the speech, aware people were still talking. I know also that something happened inside of me that I couldn't explain. The nerves were there, yes. However, I was somehow transported to a different level. The words that came, the thoughts and feelings that were enveloping me like a warm blanket, were not those I had prepared. I no longer looked down at the paper but spoke from my heart, looking out to the sea of strangers and reaching into their hearts.

As I shared my son, his wish, his legacy, and laid the story bare, the Great Hall fell so silent you could hear a pin drop. I went over my allotted time, and no one noticed or cared.

People reached for their napkins to wipe away tears, smiling at the same time. Men would occasionally cough or sigh, trying to keep it together.

As I neared the end, I knew I had reached them.

I wiped my own tears and thanked them for their generosity and for listening. Feeling Ollie's presence, I knew I had done a good job.

Breaking the silence, people stood to applaud.

Looking in the direction of my family, I invited them onstage.

As the cheers subsided, the chairman of Metra Railways, Jeffrey Ladd, approached to give his closing speech. While my family stood there, united in our joy from Ollie's impact, Mr. Ladd eloquently thanked me and the patrons.

Turning to us, he said, "Well, Debi, in closing we have a surprise for you and your family. It was indeed a great honor to be able to grant Ollie his wish to be a train driver. However, it recently came to my attention that Ollie's true wish was to actually *be* a train." He paused. "And as we know, the Make-A-Wish Foundation always looks to ensure every child has their *true* wish granted. With the assistance of BNSF, it gives me great pleasure to inform you that we, and myself personally, are honored to be able to be a part of that wish. So today as we speak, we have sitting on track number three our newest locomotive, Engine 401. And if you look at the screen behind you, you'll see that Metra announces with great pride this engine will bear the name of your son Oliver 'Ollie' Tibbles. He is indeed what he always knew he would be—a train."

From the audience, gasps were quickly followed by thunderous applause. We joined them with many repetitions of, "Oh my God," as we stood there in utter disbelief. We were otherwise speechless and emotional. As we hugged each other, the chairman continued, revealing it was the first time in rail history that a train had been named after a child.

I would later learn it was rare for a train to be named after a person at all, as most locomotives were named after towns and cities.

Engine 401, Mr. Ladd explained, would be in service for approximately fifty years, daily ferrying passengers up and down the Aurora to Chicago line, the same one from Ollie's wish day.

Following the event, Debbie Purcell would tell me that following her reading of my story, she'd had a profound moment on her way to work. Sitting in traffic just outside of Chicago, she had looked toward the railroad tracks and seen what she always had on her daily trip to the foundation's offices: a Metra passenger train. Only this time she had what she described was a vision of sorts. As she looked at the train and at the engine, she could see Ollie's name written on the side. This moment, she would later recall with me, left her feeling breathless and her skin tingling, an experience I knew only too well. Remembering Ollie's innocent prophecy of being a train when he grew up, she felt strongly this was her own sign and that she must act upon it. She had spoken on behalf of the Make-A-Wish Foundation to Metra, and many secret meetings had taken place to get us to this moment.

The events and synchronicities on this journey were the stuff of movies, the ones you watch with families at Christmas on Lifetime, the kind that has book clubs talking in earnest, some believing, some not.

Many have seen Ollie's train since that magical unveiling. In true railroad fashion, he is spreading his message of love, hope, and strength, and people are inspired.

If you happen to see him as he flies across the tracks, I invite you to wave, and you might just feel him wave back.

"I'm going to be a train."

And Ollie smiles.

Postscript

Since the Wish Ball in 2005, my journey and that of my family carries on. I returned to teaching later the same year, using the platform to share my son's legacy: the power we have inside of us, the *light*, and how with love we truly can overcome any obstacles in life and actually create the life we *want*.

I've always said that it's not the pot of gold at the end of the rainbow that counts. It's the rainbow itself—traveling your path, *believing* in it, believing in *you*—and when you do, you find true joy in your life.

Today, Ollie's train affects all who board it or see it pass by. Testament to that are the e-mails I receive daily from people whose lives are affected by Engine 401 and the little boy who knew he would be a train. To know his train will be in service for fifty years just blows my mind. His legacy will continue. For my children and my children's children, this knowledge makes me grateful beyond measure. I smile knowing his love is spreading in just the way he said it would.

Pete and I eventually parted, and he is now happily re-married. He remains a constant in the lives of our children, who are equally thriving despite the challenges they have endured. Their brother lives on inside them, and recently George, now eighteen, shared thoughts of his brother and Ollie's impact on him.

There is nothing worse than losing someone you love. I don't know whether we are all ignorant to the fact that life can end at any moment or that we just avoid the topic until we are faced with it. Nonetheless, it's disgusting to think of all the time we have wasted pushing loved ones away. I lost my brother, Ollie, and miss him terribly every blurry morning I open my eyes and every sickening night I close them. Walking these streets while he was never given the chance hurts me even more. The connection between two brothers is not one that can be replicated. The bond there is unique, and I am forever grateful to have been given seven years of it with one of the most astonishing human beings this world has seen. Even without years of experience or knowledge of life, Ollie was wise and knew what it meant to be alive. He was genuinely happy, even knowing he would die at a young age. He tried to make others happy too. Even though everybody wanted to help him, he didn't need it. Ollie knew what was going to happen, and he made the decision to not break down over it. He chose to be happy, and that to me is amazing. He was so strong, and it makes me feel awful because nobody like that should have to die so young. I miss him and his positive radiation, and I wish I had taken advantage of it more. People today don't appreciate family or even their friends because we are so oblivious to how quickly circumstances can turn. Ollie has taught me numerous things, both while alive and while deceased. People have the power to overcome any obstacle put in their way and also are given the privilege of others who love them, so take advantage of their being. Don't fret over the small issues, and make a smile out of every day. Ollie did, and he died a happy child. He will always be my brother. That connection will never be broken, and I hope to one day live and love as he did.

George writes for his high school newspaper and is planning to enter into journalism. I've told him he can do whatever he wants in life, yet somehow I think he already knows it.

Jess also shared some thoughts in part of a paper she was writing for English.

I can remember walking through the hallways of junior high school, acting like nothing was wrong. I had a lump in my throat and fought back tears, but I hid it well and put a smile on my face. My fellow peers and teachers all watched with sympathetic eyes and faint smiles. They all knew my brother had died but didn't know how to approach me. I hated it—hated the sympathy, didn't want to talk to anyone and just wanted to be left alone, yet this was close to impossible and to this day I don't know how I did it because behind the fake smile was a broken girl who had no idea what to do with her emotions. My mind was racing 24-7, but I always knew how to hide it, which I think confused my parents, like they thought I didn't care because of the way I acted when in reality I was dying inside.

My little brother was an amazing little boy. He was one of those cute little boys that the moment you met him, you fell in love. He cared about so many people and always put others before himself. Ollie struggled with cancer for two years and met many doctors and nurses along the way. I can say with pride that he touched every single one of those people and will stay in their hearts forever. The one thing that has kept me going over the years is that he is over the struggle, free of pain, and will always be remembered and loved by many, many people. Yes, I wish it had never happened to him. Yes, I wish he was still with us. And yes, I wish he had lived longer than just seven years. Yet at the same time, without even being here, he is making a difference in the world, touching people's hearts and helping others. That is what gets me out of bed every day. Ollie has changed my life forever, and I will always cherish the memories and feel proud of my strong, caring brother who to me is a true hero. He's my hero and always will be.

Jess entered college this year and is studying psychology. Many of Jess's friends reach out to her, drawn by her caring, sensitive nature and maturity, part of which I know is due to the challenges she has faced. Of course, she is still only twenty-one. Despite her wise soul, she still acts her age on occasion, raising my eyebrows, and I thank God she does.

❧

I left the fitness industry for a while to focus on public speaking engagements both at live events and also via the airwaves, most recently with Martha Stewart Living Radio and with my dear friend John St. Augustine, former senior producer for Oprah Radio. How we met was a culmination of those "God winks" moments.

I continue to write and am currently working on my second book, *Good Grief.* My passion for fitness remains, however, and I still enjoy teaching part-time and using my platform to spread Ollie's message.

I met and fell in love with my partner, Jennifer, five years ago. She lights my world, and I feel truly blessed. Love, *true* love, doesn't care about the color of your skin or what sex you are. Real love just happens. I think we make love difficult by questioning it and having expectations of it and each other. Love is just love. It's that simple.

In 2010, I reconnected with my dad. It had been eight years since we'd spoken or seen each other, and thanks to the kindness of a friend, I was able to make the trip to England to see him. I did not tell him I was coming and just turned up on his seventieth birthday. The look on his face was priceless. He told me it was the best birthday gift a father could have. It takes guts and a compassionate heart to forgive, and we both did. Why? Because that is the power of love, a lesson passed to me by my son. Today my father and I are the closest we have ever been and proof indeed that it is never too late.

The past ten years have changed my life. I am here via the legacy of my son: to inspire and lead others to better lives and to open their eyes to the truth that once you embrace love, anything is possible. That no matter the obstacles we face in life, we need not be afraid.

After Ollie passed, one of his school friends, who

was nine years old at the time, presented an acrostic poem to me that looked like this:

Ollie's
Love
Lives
In
Everyone
    Love,
    Lexie XXXXXXX

Children are always the most insightful teachers. George, Jess, I, and so many people learned our most important life lessons from Ollie. Ollie was my greatest teacher, a precious son, and the most courageous, kindest human being I ever knew. I will always be grateful for the seven glorious years I had with him. I feel truly honored to be his mother and am proud to do as he asked. This *is* my path, and I embrace it with love and grace, wherever it may lead.

Ollie's Spirit

There's a train in the sky
Who never questioned why,
Who knew what he would be,
Who knew that I would see.
There's a train in the sky,
whose love is not mine alone.
His love is for everyone,
to bring you all back home.

Acknowledgments

I never imagined I'd be in this spot where I have the opportunity to thank all those who have supported me throughout this journey. At the same time, it's every author's nightmare: I hope I don't miss anyone. I have been blessed with meeting so many amazing individuals who jumped aboard this ride and helped this book come to fruition. So with that said, here we go!

First to my children, Jessica, George, and Ollie, without whom this book would never have been written. For Ollie, who was the inspiration and instigator and who continues to inspire me daily. For Jessica and George, who as children taught me many lessons while overcoming challenges few adults have had to endure. I thank you both for allowing me to be the mother for your brother when he needed me more, in the times I was not there for you, for the love and courage you have both shown, and for your continued support of me. I am thankful and proud you are my children.

To Pete, the father of my children who holds a special place in my heart. To my family back in England: I thank you and miss you. To Jen, who endured the tears, sweat, and joy during the many rewrites and reconnected me to the wonders of nature.

To Dr. Stewart Goldman of Children's Memorial Hospital, Chicago, a brilliant scientist, unique human being, and friend: for your compassion, hope, and silly jokes, and for giving Ollie his childhood back. Heartfelt thanks to Dr. Haywood and all the staff at Great Ormond Street Hospital, London, for their dedication to our son and giving us hope when we needed it most. Deepest thanks to all the staff at Children's, including Kristin Leigh Hughes and Erin Perkins, for their staunch support.

And a special shout-out to Eric and Kathy from 101.9 FM, The Mix, and the producers for their tireless fund-raising efforts in supporting Children's Memorial. Thank you to Debbie Purcell of the Make-A-Wish Foundation of Illinois and to Metra along with BNSF Railway Company, who believed in a child's dream, and to Ginny Weissman for seeing my own. I will always be grateful.

Many thanks to my publisher, Medallion Press,

OLLIE TIBBLES: THE BOY WHO BECAME A TRAIN

and to their president, Adam Mock, for a conversation in my dressing gown (that's a housecoat, to many of you) that I will never forget and for sharing and believing in Ollie Fever. Fond thanks to my editor, Emily Steele, for keeping the integrity and the Britishness of this story yet mostly for the kind comments during the rewrites; deeply touched.

Deepest thanks to my dear friend John St. Augustine, creator of Oprah Radio, whose friendship I treasure. God bless you, John, for the moments that matter and many more to come. It's a bloody setup!

Thanks to Tom of Tom Martin Media for his tireless time and energy given freely in support of this book and for the friendship. Tom, it's a pleasure to know you.

A big thank-you to my friend and personal photographer, Mark Saunders, whose ability to see me and the moments we all feel is uncanny. To photographer Andrew Taylor for capturing the essence and magic of Ollie along with precious keepsakes to last a lifetime. Thank you, my friend.

Deepest thanks and gratitude to Kate and Michael Marcey for the gift I will always treasure and your wonderful friendship. God bless you both.

Fond thanks to Michael Kay and Victoria Gaither of At Home with Victoria Blog Talk Radio, for your friendship and loyal support.

Special thanks to all the people I have met and

known within the fitness industry over the years, where my platform as a teacher allowed me to grow. To my members, whose love and support remain in my heart.

Special thanks to all my friends—you know who you are—for being there. I thank you and love you. And a huge shout-out to my Facebook friends, many of whom know me yet don't know me and love me regardless, proof of the pudding that even out in cyberspace, love knows no bounds.

Last yet by no means least, I thank the Universe for all my life, for all these moments, for the people who helped shape them, and finally for peace in my heart.

God bless you.

MEDALLION
P R E S S

Be in the know on the latest Medallion Press news by
becoming a Medallion Press Insider!

<u>As an Insider you'll receive:</u>
· Our FREE expanded monthly newsletter, giving you more insight into
Medallion Press
· Advanced press releases and breaking news
· Greater access to all your favorite Medallion authors

Joining is easy. Just visit our website at
<u>www.medallionmediagroup.com</u> and click on
Super Cool E-blast next to the social media buttons.

medallionmediagroup.com

MEDALLION

P   R   E   S   S

Want to know what's going on with your favorite author or
what new releases are coming from Medallion Press?

Now you can receive breaking news, updates, and more from
Medallion Press straight to your cell phone, e-mail, instant
messenger, or Facebook!

Sign up now at www.twitter.com/MedallionPress to stay on top of all
the happenings in and around Medallion Press.

For more information
about other great titles from
Medallion Press, visit

medallionmediagroup.com